Thomas Meyrick

Lives Of The Early Popes

St. Peter To St. Silvester

Thomas Meyrick

Lives Of The Early Popes
St. Peter To St. Silvester

ISBN/EAN: 9783743335851

Manufactured in Europe, USA, Canada, Australia, Japa

Cover: Foto ©Lupo / pixelio.de

Manufactured and distributed by brebook publishing software (www.brebook.com)

Thomas Meyrick

Lives Of The Early Popes

LIVES OF THE EARLY POPES.

St. Peter to St. Silvester.

BY THE

REV. THOMAS MEYRICK, M.A.,

AUTHOR OF "THE LIFE OF ST. WENEFRED," ETC.

LONDON:

R. WASHBOURNE, 18 PATERNOSTER ROW.

1878.

THIS LITTLE VOLUME OF THE FIRST SERIES

OF THE POPES' LIVES

𝔍𝔰 𝔍𝔫𝔰𝔠𝔯𝔦𝔟𝔢𝔡

To WILLIAM HERBERT, ESQ., OF CLYTHA,

UNDER WHOSE HONOURED ROOF

IT WAS COMPLETED.

PREFACE.

THE object of this work is to give a simple con-
secutive account of the lives of the early Popes. It
is taken partly from Bartholomew Platina, of Cre-
mona, who wrote by order of Pope Sixtus IV., and
dedicated his work to him, and partly from Alphonsus
Ciaconi, a Dominican, supplemented by Father Oldoin,
S.J., with occasional reference to Baronius and others.
In his preface, Platina justly observes that the true
history of illustrious men is a great benefit to mankind, enabling posterity to converse with men of past
times, to take counsel with them, and imitate their
virtues as if they saw them living. It is a study
that contributes to true civilization and practical
progress in every department of knowledge, so much
so, that authors who have well described the actions
of celebrated men, are reckoned among the first of
mankind for wisdom and intelligence. But above
all, the lives of the Popes are calculated to give
honour to God, glory to the Church, and good examples
to men, for it is they who have been the keepers of
the Christian commonwealth, and by their labours

and sufferings have preserved it upon earth under God, until now, without stain and immaculate. They form a race of princes or kings, whose succession is unbroken from Christ our Lord, and on the throne established by Him, the chair of St. Peter. Scarce any writer, says Platina, has taken pains to compose a history of them with any pretence to elegance and beauty, excepting one of themselves, Pope Damasus, who was an accomplished scholar. In modern times Protestants have attempted to write their histories, but from their point of view the Popes are for the most part actuated by such motives as those which influence ordinary men and politicians. Hence to read them is a painful task. Non-Catholic writers cannot form in their minds the focus from which to throw a clear light on the objects they present to view. As St. Teresa expresses it, the "glass is broken, and the speculum, or reflective power, is all in pieces."

In traversing the course of remote ages less commonly known, this simple work will be acceptable to those who wish to form a summary acquaintance with the grand personages who in ancient times have filled the majestic place of the Princes of the Church in the chair of St. Peter.

Their lives necessarily imply a notice of contemporary emperors and kings or other leading men of the times, as oppressors or favourers of Christianity. At first they were the persecutors of the Church, and afterwards its servants or nursing fathers, or not unfrequently its disobedient children or its tyrannical oppressors.

Consequently, in perusing the lives of the heads of Christendom, we must obtain a general history of all that is most momentous in the civilized world, so that this is a sufficient commendation of the work to all who desire the diffusion of useful Christian knowledge. It has no pretension to be more than a brief popular compilation.

It may seem strange to some that comparatively little is recorded of many Popes, and so much is said of contemporary emperors; but in the scene of history the prominent personages are those who figure as dominant in the world. The Popes in the early times were hidden; they had no celebrated historians. The great writers of the world speak of their own great men, of whom they make a wonder, and in a certain sense they are wonderful, otherwise they would not be made much of, and they rise and fall, come and go upon the stage like, in the visions of the Apocalypse, beast rises after beast, at whom the world for a time wonders. The victims of their cruelty and persecution are comparatively insignificant or unpleasant subjects for historians, and they serve only as a foil to set off the importance of these heroes among men.

Yet it is these humble men of suffering and patience in the truth who are the real centre of the world's history. It was with the Saints and their lives that the history of the world dealt in the Book of Books before Christ came, though the acts of the kings of Judah and of Israel are more prominently recorded. It is still with the Saints' lives that Christian history deals since Christ came.

In our own day, the prominent personages who have attracted the admiration of the world have been an iron-souled politician, a successful bravo, a jovial king, while saintly pontiffs, more important without comparison in reality, are wronged with impunity, and their wrongs passed over in silence, or noted only with a passing sneer.

This first little volume may stand alone as giving the early Popes down to the time of Constantine, or may be followed by others according as its usefulness and success may determine.

CONTENTS.

xii Contents.

THE LIVES OF THE EARLY POPES.

CHAPTER I.

ST. PETER.

FIRST PERSECUTION UNDER NERO.

JESUS is the name of the Saviour of men; Christ
the name of their King; for by their anointing, the
kings of the people of God were distinguished, as
other earthly monarchs by the purple. Priests and
prophets were also anointed; but The Anointed, or
the Messia, is a King. Christ came to establish
the throne of David, and to reign upon the earth.

After His death and resurrection, which are the
foundations of the Christian faith, the Apostles
received the Holy Ghost on the day of Pentecost,
and declared to assembled nations at Jersusalem the
Passion and Resurrection of the Son of God. Peter
and John, fishermen, were the chiefs of these. The
twelve under Peter, who took the place of Christ as
shepherd of the flock, lived in poverty, receiving the
contributions of the faithful for the good of the com-
munity which they served as the ministers of God.
What remained over from the general necessities

1

and their own wants they distributed to the poor. Peter remained five years at Jerusalem, of which he ordained James the Less bishop, being assisted in the ordination by St. James and St. John, thus establishing the precedent that a bishop should be consecrated by three bishops—this fact is recorded by Pope Anacletus.

When the Apostles parted company to preach to the world, Thomas went to Persia and Scinde, Matthew to Abyssinia, Bartholomew to Bactria and Armenia, Andrew to the Scythians of the north, John to Asia Minor, where he outlived the rest to see the world Christian, and resided at Ephesus. Pontus, Galatia, Bithynia and Cappadocia fell to the lot of Peter, who in the sixth year went to Antioch, where he founded the Church, and held it as his see for seven years, during which time he often visited Jerusalem. Tiberius, and after him Caligula, were emperors at Rome. This last cruel monster was put to death in the third year of his empire, leaving, it is said, a chest of poisons so deadly, that they infected the sea into which they were thrown by command of Claudius.

In the sixth year of his Pontificate at Antioch, Peter, being at Jerusalem after the martyrdom of James, was put in prison by Herod, from which he was miraculously delivered by an angel. He then retired from Jerusalem, and took his journey to Rome, the particulars of which are given by Ciaconi from ancient sources. Going to Cesarea, he made Zachæus bishop there. From thence he passed to Sidon, Beyrout, and Tripoli; then to Ortosa, Antandrus, Aradus, and Laodicea; from Laodicea to Antioch, where he ordained Evodius bishop.

Passing from thence to Nicomedia and Ilium, he ordained Cornelius bishop and Lazarus priest, and, proceeding to Ephesus and Smyrna, crossed into Macedonia. At Philippi he ordained Olympus; at Thessalonica, Jason; at Corinth, Silanus. From Corinth he went to Sicily, and then to Naples. At Naples he cured Asprenas by a miracle, touching him with his staff, and ordained him Bishop of Naples. The Church of the Altar of St. Peter preserves the tradition of his saying Mass there. From Naples he is said to have gone by sea to Leghorn and Pisa; and so, in the second year of Claudius, he entered Rome, A.D. 45.

From this year dates the commencement of the Pontificate of Peter and the Papacy at Rome, with its Divine commission to rule upon earth, with the power of binding and loosing, and with the Keys that open and shut. Rome, as head and mistress of the known world, was naturally chosen for the seat of Heaven's vicegerent. Humble as his entrance was into the Eternal City, he came to found a kingdom to last to the world's end, and to verify the words of Christ: "Thou art Peter, and upon this rock I will build My Church, and the gates of hell shall not prevail against it. And to thee will I give the keys of the kingdom of heaven." He stayed three years in Rome; first in the Jewish quarters, in the Trastevere, and afterwards in the house of the Senator Pudens, on the Viminal. He was accompanied from Antioch by Apollinaris, Clement, Martialis, Priscus, and by Mark, either at this time or on his return to Rome from the East, which he revisited, after three years' residence in Rome, to hold the Council in Jerusalem.

The preaching of Christianity probably caused disturbance and sedition among the Jews in Rome, as a passage in Tacitus seems to imply; and Claudius the emperor gave command for the banishment of the Jews. He also repressed a tumult of the Jews, caused by some false prophets in Judea, making Cumanus procurator, in whose time thirty thousand are said to have been trampled to death in the gates of the Temple at the time of the Passover. This emperor, the uncle of Caligula, spared by him for his supposed imbecility, died poisoned by his niece Agrippina, the daughter of Germanicus, whom he unlawfully married, after an empire of thirteen years. He added Britain to the Roman Empire, and the Orkney Isles.

Peter, after preaching in the East, returned to Rome in the second year of Nero, and wrote his first Epistle, which he sent by Silvanus. At the request of the Romans, he committed to Mark the task of writing his Gospel. St. Mark, as St. Jerome relates, was a priest of the tribe of Levi, baptised by St. Peter; and in his Gospel, which had Peter's approval, he exhibits in a special manner the royal character of Christ. Sent by Peter to Egypt, he founded the Church of Alexandria, where, as Philo Judæus records, he lived in great sanctity of life, and died a martyr in the eighth year of Nero, and was succeeded by Anianus.

Apollinaris was also ordained bishop by St. Peter, and sent to Ravenna, where, having preached the Gospel, he was taken by the priests of the idols, scourged, and banished, after making many converts. Again preaching in Emilia, he was seized and banished to Asia, from whence he passed into Thrace, and finally returned to Ravenna, where he was martyred. His feast is on the 23rd of July. A list of other bishops ordained by St. Peter is given by Father Oldoin, from ancient authorities; Stachys at Byzantium, Domnio at Salona, Amasian at Tarentum, Photinus at Beneventum, Saturninus at Toulouse, Rufus at Avignon, Altinus at Orleans, Anathelon at Milan, Aristobulus in Britain, and others in France and Italy, Corsica and Sardinia.

Between the second year of Nero and the tenth, Peter preached in the West, and, according to Simeon Metaphrastes, in Britain. It is out of the compass of this work to enter into questions that involve a large amount of research and learning, for it would swell into an ecclesiastical history; but this much seems certain, that the faith was preached in Britain, as in the rest of the world, in the time of the Apostles. There is also sufficient evidence that St. Joseph of Arimathea penetrated to the far west of the island, and founded the mother church of Glastonbury.

During his absence from Rome, Linus, ordained bishop of the city, and Cletus, of the suburban district, acted in St. Peter's stead. They seem, moreover, to have acted as coadjutors in attending to the wants of the Christians in Rome and the strangers who came there. Clement was Peter's assistant deacon, and seems to have been his favourite disciple. These three may be called the germ of the future cardinals.

St. Paul, born in the city of Giscala, of the tribe of Benjamin, upon the capture of his native town by the Romans, went with his mother to live at Tarsus, in Cilicia, from whence he came to Jerusalem, to study the law under Gamaliel. He took the name of Paul from Sergius Paulus, pro-consul of Cyprus, whom he converted. Returning to Jerusalem with Barnabas after his missionary labours, he was there elected and ordained apostle of the Gentiles by Peter, James, and John. In the second year of Nero, A.D. 58, he was sent prisoner to Rome with Aristarchus, his fellow-captive, and, as a Roman citizen, allowed some liberty in his captivity, disputing with the Jews, and detained a prisoner two years. At length, being liberated, he preached in the western world, and probably to its extremities, in Spain, Gaul, and Britain, as St. Peter is said to have done.

In the seventh year of Nero, James the Just, called the Brother of the Lord, was martyred by the Jews. Hegesippus, who lived shortly after the Apostolic age, says of him: "That he was a Nazarite, sanctified from his mother's womb, never tasting wine or flesh, or touched by razor, nor using bath or unguent, and was clothed in linen. He was allowed ingress into the Holy of Holies, and his knees were hardened like a camel's, by constant prayer." In the absence of Festus the governor, at his retirement from the province, to be succeeded by Albinus, Annas the high priest, the son of Anna, bid him deny Christ to be the Son of God, which when he refused, he **was** sentenced to be stoned to death. He **was** placed upon a pinnacle or balcony of the Temple, to be heard by the populace, when, instead of abjuring, he proclaimed the faith, and was thrown down. Being still alive, and lifting up his hands to pray for his persecutors, he was struck by a fuller's club, and expired. Josephus says of him that the repute of his sanctity was so great, that it was commonly thought that on account of his unjust death Jerusalem was destroyed. It was to James that Our Lord is said to have appeared after His resurrection, to comfort him after His passion, since which he had eaten no food, and taking bread, blessed it and broke, saying, " Eat thy bread, My brother, because the Son of Man is risen from the dead." He was Bishop of Jerusalem to the year 63, the seventh of Nero, and his sepulchre was to be seen on the spot where he fell when thrown from the Temple until the time of Hadrian.

Barnabas of Cyprus also died by martyrdom before St. Peter. Elected with St. Paul apostle of the Gentiles, he wrote an epistle, which is not admitted to the canon of Scripture. Separating from Paul on account of the disciple Mark, whom he took with him to Cyprus, he died there preaching the faith and crowned with martyrdom.

About the tenth year of Nero, St. Peter returned to Rome, to comfort the Christians in their dreadful persecution. Nero is said to have set fire to the city in a mad freak, to witness the conflagration as exhibiting the burning of Troy, and at the same time with the intent of destroying the old and tortuous narrow streets of Rome. Out of the whole fourteen regions of the city, seven were completely destroyed and three others partially. The conflagration is said to have continued nine days. Accusation was made against the Christians of having fired the city, and they were apprehended in numbers. Some were wrapped in beasts' skins and baited with dogs; others clothed in garments smeared with pitch, to be slowly burnt alive, and serve as torches by night. Few men have exceeded Nero in cruelty and wanton wickedness. He sought victims not only among Christians, but in all men of note, and of these were Seneca, his own preceptor, and Lucan the poet. He murdered his own mother Agrippina, and his wife Octavia. His luxury was so great, that he bathed in liquid odoriferous unguents, and fished with nets of woven gold. He built magnificent public baths, and a palace called the Golden House, the galleries of which extended three miles. The first great persecution raised by him began the series of battles with the Church, in which the armies of hell endeavoured to extinguish the light of Christianity. The great anti-Christian monster was lashed into paroxysms of fury from time to time in defence of the old seat of iniquity in which he had reigned, and his rage fell upon the Popes, the successors of Peter.

In the twelfth year of Nero, not long before he suffered, Peter wrote his second Epistle to the Churches from this Babylon. He knew that his death was drawing near, and he predicted the destruction of Jerusalem, which in a brief time was to ensue. His contest with Simon Magus occurred at this time. That arch-impostor and apostate had wandered with his companion, Selene, to the world's city of corruption, and, competing with Peter in power of performing miracles, made a dead boy move by magic arts, but could not raise him to life. Peter resuscitated him in the Name of Jesus. Simon then challenged Peter to fly in the air from the Capitoline Mount to the Aventine in the sight of the people. At Peter's prayer the magician fell in his flight, broke his leg, and being carried by his satellites to Aricia, there died of vexation.

By this circumstance, or by the splendour of his sanctity and the veneration in which he was held, Peter awakened the notice and jealousy of Nero. He was seized, together with St. Paul, who had come to Rome in the same perilous time of persecution. According to the general tradition, Peter was thrown into the Mamertine prison, where he baptised the gaoler and was liberated by him, or, as others say, before he was taken, by the counsel of the Christians he departed from Rome by the Capenian Gate, and, as Hegesippus, Ambrose, and Gregory relate, Christ appeared to him as if on His way to Rome. Peter said, "Domine, quo vadis? Lord, whither goest Thou?" And the Lord said, "I go to Rome again to be crucified." Then Peter knew that his time was come, and the manner of his death according to Christ's prophecy, and returned to Rome to die. He had chosen Clement as his successor, to whom

he committed the care of the Church in his stead,
taking him by the hand and saying, " I give thee
the same power of binding and loosing which Christ
gave to me : despising all things of the world and
the flesh, by prayer and preaching attend as a good
pastor to the salvation of men."

Peter, condemned to a servile death, was crucified,
and, at his own request, with his head downwards,
as he said he was unworthy to be crucified in the
same manner as his Lord and master, Jesus Christ.
The place of his martyrdom was that summit of the
Janiculum which is called from it the Golden or
Montorio.   Clement, with his disciples, Marcellus
and Apuleius, received his body and buried it at the
gardens of Nero on the Vatican, by the temple of
Apollo.   St. Paul, sentenced as a Roman citizen to
be beheaded, was martyred on the same day on the
Ostian road, and was buried there.   It is superfluous,
in the face of the consent of antiquity and all tradition, to raise the modern question of St. Peter having
been at Rome.   As Caius says, writing against Pro-
culus : " I can point out to you the tokens of the
victory of the two Apostles, for if you go upon the
royal road which leads to the Vatican, or upon the
Ostian road, you will find the trophies of the two
who most certainly founded this Church of Rome—
Peter and Paul."

Nicephorus gives the personal appearance of St.
Peter.   He was rather tall and of a slender make ;
his face pale, and his complexion remarkably fair ;
his hair and beard were short, crisp, and curly ; his
eyes dark and bloodshot with much weeping ; his

nose of moderate length, not aquiline, but slightly turned up. The same author describes St. Paul, and is confirmed by St. John Chrysostom and Lucian. He was small in stature, which he made still less by an habitual stoop in his carriage ; his face fair, his head small, and he appeared rather older than his years ; his eyes were remarkably beautiful in expression ; his eyebrows arched, his nose rather long, delicate, and aquiline ; his beard very long and full. This description agrees with the traditional likenesses, and those depicted on the glass plates or patens found in the catacombs.

The bodies of the Apostles lay undisturbed until some emissaries from the East attempted to carry them off. In this they so far succeeded as to convey them out of the city ; but being suddenly overtaken and terrified by a storm of thunder and lightning, they cast the bodies into a cemetery on the Appian Way, called from thence "ad Catacumbas." From this again they were removed after a lapse of time, as some authors say, by St. Cornelius, or, according to others, by St. Silvester, who at least more accurately divided the relics, giving the larger bones to St. Peter and the lesser to St. Paul, and replaced them respectively in the Vatican and on the Ostian road. St. Peter held the Pontificate in Rome twenty-four years, five months, and eleven days, in round numbers, twenty-five years. If we add to these the seven years at Antioch, the years of Peter may be reckoned as thirty-two.

Nero did not long survive the death of the Apostles. Condemned by the public voice to be dragged through the streets under the fork, and scourged to death, and his body to be thrown into the Tiber, he fled in fear to a suburban villa, where he put an end to his own life with a razor in his thirty-second year.   The great persecutors for the most part died in a fearful manner, as a warning to all men, like Antiochus Epiphanes, Herod the Great, and Herod Agrippa.

CHAPTER II.

SECOND PERSECUTION UNDER DOMITIAN.

A.D. 69.—Romulus and Remus, suckled by a wolf, founded Rome in blood—a brother slain by a brother's hand. St. Peter and Paul founded the Christian Church, and inaugurated the reign of Christ on earth, in love and amity, giving their lives for Him and the salvation of men. Although Clement, by appointment of Peter, had the right of succession, he gave an example of unambitious modesty by yielding the place to Linus, the co-adjutor of St. Peter in the city. By his refusal, he obliged Linus and Cletus to be Popes before him.

Accordingly Linus, a Tuscan of the town of Volaterra, the son of Herculanus, succeeded Peter, and was Pontiff from the last year of Nero to the time of Vespasian, from the consulate of Scipio and Saturninus, to the consulate of Capito and Ruffus. Linus, says Father Oldoin, came to Rome for the sake of study at the age of twenty-two, and lived in the house of Fabius, his father's friend. He left all to follow St. Peter, and was sent by him on a mission to Gaul, where he converted the tribune Onasius, and founded a church in honour of the protomartyr

Stephen. He is said to have founded also St.
Stephano in Rotondo, in Rome. Ordained bishop
by St. Peter, he acted as his vicar. He is mentioned
by St. Paul in his Second Epistle to Timothy,
" Linus and Eubulus, etc., salute you."

In the time of Linus, Jerusalem was destroyed.
According to Josephus, a million of Jews were
either slain or otherwise perished in the city, or
were led into captivity and sold, being gathered from
all parts of the world to keep the Pasch. Thus
they received retribution for the death of Christ
their king, whom they slew at the time of the Passover, being collected there as into a vast prison, to
suffer the death of malefactors, and great numbers
were crucified. Linus baptised Nazarius, the son
of Africanus and Perpetua, who went into Cisalpine
Gaul, and was Apostle of Piedmont. He was
accompanied by the boy Celsus, who endured with
him many torments, from which they were delivered
by miracle. Preaching the faith at Milan, they
suffered martyrdom in that city, and were buried
outside of the Roman gate, where their bodies were
afterwards discovered by St. Ambrose, and translated with honour.

In the fifth year of Linus, St. Bartholomew
suffered in Armenia, flayed alive ; and in the
seventh, St. Thomas transfixed by a Brahmin's
spear in India, at Calamina.

The empire was convulsed after the death of
Nero. Three emperors followed in quick succession.
Galba, an old commander coming from Spain, was
soon murdered by the Prætorian Guard for refusing

a donative, and his headless corpse trodden down in the Forum. Otho perished by his own hand in desperation upon news of the defeat of his legions by Vitellius. The German army, led down into Italy by Vitellius, at the cost of sanguinary battles, in one of which forty thousand were left dead upon the field, made him master of Rome for a brief time, in spite of the Prætorian Guard. He feasted for a little while, and then, dragged from a vile hiding-place in the palace, was beaten to death by the populace, and his huge body cast into the Tiber, upon the news of the approach of the legions of Vespasian from the East.

Linus wrote the Acts of the Martyrdom of SS. Peter and Paul, and the Contest of St. Peter with Simon Magus ; but how far these are genuine as they exist is doubtful. He added the "Communicantes" to the Liturgy, and commanded women to veil their heads in the church. He was powerful in chasing demons from the bodies of the possessed, and raised even the dead to life. He was condemned to death by the consul, Saturninus, whose daughter he had delivered from the devil. Besides Nazarius and Celsus, Martialis, the apostle of Gaul, Processus and Martinianus, and many others, were martyrs in his time. He twice held ordinations, creating eleven bishops and eighteen priests, and after a pontificate of ten, or, as some say, eleven years, was buried in the Vatican beside St. Peter, on the 23rd of September, A.D. 79 or 80.

A.D. 80.—Cletus, a Roman, the son of Æmilian, of the Patrician quarter, was obliged to fill the chair of Peter against his will, Clement again refusing it. He was esteemed by others most worthy of the dignity for holiness and wisdom, but in his own eyes he deemed himself unworthy. He was Pope during the empire of Vespasian and Titus to the times of Domitian; from the seventh consulate of Vespasian and fifth of Domitian, to the consulship of Domitian and Ruffus, as Pope Damasus records.

After the taking of Jerusalem, Titus and Vespasian triumphed, riding in the same chariot, and Domitian followed on a white horse. The Arch of Titus remains, showing the tables of the law and the seven-branched candlestick borne in the procession. Vespasian was a merciful and clement emperor, and was a good prince, except for his love of gathering money, in which, however, he exacted nothing unjustly. He expended the money he collected in completing the Temple of Peace in the Forum, and beginning the Colosseum or Flavian Amphitheatre. His son, Titus, was as gentle in peace as he was brave in war, and so liberal, that he refused no man's request, saying that the face of the prince should send every man glad away. He counted the day lost in which he had done no man a favour. When he finished building his public baths, and the great Amphitheatre, he displayed his magnificence by a show or hunt of five thousand wild beasts. He was called the darling of mankind, but the mean and ill-favoured countenances of Vespasian and Titus, as seen upon their coins, display features hardly in keeping with the extravagant eulogies of their flatterers.

In the first year of Cletus, A.D. 80, the fearful eruption of Vesuvius burst forth which buried Herculaneum and Pompeii. The air was filled with ashes, which were carried by the wind to the coasts of Africa and Syria, and darkened the heavens at Rome. We have by this circumstance preserved to us many ocular testimonies of the refinement, luxury, and domestic habits of heathen life. Their method of taking the bath, and their shows of gladiators, with their various manner of combat in those cruel exhibitions, are represented on the walls of the exhumed houses of Pompeii. Some idea is also given of the elegance of their musical entertainments and theatricals.

In the Pontificate of Cletus, St. Luke the Evangelist died a martyr in Greece at the age of eighty-three. St. Gregory of Nazianzen speaks of his martyrdom, and Nicephorus says that he was crucified on an olive tree. His body was translated afterwards to Constantinople with the relics of St. Andrew, in the time of Constantius. About the same period St. Philip, after twenty years' preaching in Russia, where he planted the faith, returned to Asia, and died a martyr at Hierapolis, in Phrygia. By some he is called the Apostle, by others Philip the Deacon.

The second great persecution began under Domitian. This cruel emperor soon caused the happy memory of Vespasian and Titus to be forgotten. He was so wantonly cruel, that he went by the name of a second Nero, and he claimed honours as a god. Cletus was martyred, and in the same year, A.D. 92,

2

Baronius places the living martyrdom of St. John the Evangelist, who was sent by the proconsul of Asia a prisoner on the charge of impiety to Rome, and put, by command of Domitian, into a caldron of boiling oil, from which he came forth more vigorous. Many martyrs suffered at this time, amongst whom was Flavia Domitilla, niece of the consul Clement. She was first banished to an isle of Pontus for the confession of the faith, and afterwards burned in her house. Nereus and Achilleus suffered with her. The priest Nicomedes, who had buried the martyred virgin Felicula, was beaten to death with loaded whips, and buried on the Nomentan Way near the walls. St. Timothy and Titus also suffered under Domitian, and the family of David was commanded to be sought for and exterminated.

Cletus ordained twenty-five priests, and held the Pontificate twelve years. He was buried near the body of St. Peter, on the 26th of April, A.D. 92.

A.D. 92.—After an interval of twenty days, Clement was enthroned in the chair of Peter, to which, as has been said above, he had a right of succession by the appointment of Peter himself; but he chose to yield to Linus and Cletus, the coadjutor bishops of the apostle. That Clement was the fourth Bishop of Rome is plain from the words of St. Jerome: "Linus was the second, Cletus the third, Clement the fourth Bishop of Rome." He was by birth a Roman, the son of Faustinus, of the region of the Cœlian Mount, an early convert of St. Peter and a faithful companion of the apostle. He may also be the same who is spoken of by St. Paul as his coadjutor in his letter to the Philippians, and of whom it is said that his name is written in the book of life. But some say that this is another Clement. He was ordained by St. Peter, first as his assistant deacon, and afterwards as bishop.

Clement was a great saint and a great Pope. He translated the Epistle of St. Paul to the Hebrews into Greek, and when Pope he wrote a letter to the Corinthians, fragments of which have been preserved, to put an end to a schism. It is written with authority in the name of the Church of Rome, and is the first instance of the paternal care of the See of Peter over all the Churches after the Epistle of St. Peter himself. In style it resembles St. Paul, which makes it more probable that he was a companion of that apostle as well as St. Peter, and styled by him his coadjutor. It is quoted by Justin Martyr, St. Basil, and St. Athanasius, and, as Eusebius affirms, was read in the early churches. A second epistle is also attributed to him, and other letters, two of which are to the Bishop of Jerusalem, in one of which he says, " When Simon Peter knew that the end of his life drew high, having assembled the brethren in a council, he took me by the hand and said, ' I appoint this companion of mine, who was from the first ever faithful to me since I came to Rome, the bishop of this city.' "

If this passage be genuine—and with little doubt it records a fact—it could not have been written to St. James, Bishop of Jerusalem by Clement as Pope, for St. James died before St. Peter. It might have been to his successor, who was also a relative of Our

Lord. According to Eusebius, he wrote the disputation between Peter and Appion, and his eight books of Apostolical Constitutions were revered by antiquity, being reckoned by the Abyssinians among the canonical Scriptures. His memoirs of St. Peter have been falsified, as he himself says in one of his Epistles.

The evangelist St. John was still living in Clement's time, and, exiled to the Isle of Patmos by Domitian, saw and wrote the visions of the Apocalypse. When Domitian died, in the midst of his persecution of the Church, murdered in his palace, in the fifteenth year of his empire, his acts were rescinded by Nerva, and St. John returned to Ephesus, where he survived to the time of Trajan, dying at the age of ninety-three, according to Baronius, A.D. 101. By some it is believed that his body was assumed into heaven, and that there are no relics of it.

Nerva was chosen emperor when past seventy years of age, and reigned only one year and four months. He was a just and clement prince, annulling the persecuting laws, so that many Christians returned from exile and recovered their goods. He was succeeded by Trajan, his adopted son, surnamed Crinitus, or the long-haired, a Spaniard renowned for his moderation, courteous manners, and military glory. He greatly extended the empire, bringing the Germans beyond the Rhine to peace with the Romans, subjugating the Dacians and other nations north of the Danube; he made new provinces on the Euphrates and Tigris, conquering and holding

Armenia, Assyria, Mesopotamia, Ctesiphon, and Babylon, pushed the confines of the empire to India, and built a fleet upon the Erythræan Sea to carry his arms to the coasts of the far East. Still, with all his noble qualities, wise, generous, and prudent, with many great gifts, he was a heathen, and a persecutor of the faith.

Clement, by his venerable sanctity and august character, was making many converts to the faith, amongst whom Sisinnius, a familiar friend of Nerva, had received baptism, when he was accused before Trajan by P. Tarquinius, custodian of the religious rites, and Mamertinus, prefect of the city. He was sentenced to be banished to the Tauric Chersonese, now the Crimea. Deported thither, he found two thousand Christians condemned to labour in the marble quarries. Such was the common fate of the early Christian confessors; and, in later times, to add to the barbarity of their treatment, the sinews of one foot were cauterized, to ensure their captivity and enhance their sufferings. These living martyrs were in want of water, which they had to bring from a distance of six miles. Clement prayed, and beheld a lamb standing on a hill, from whose right foot striking the ground a miraculous spring arose, with which they were supplied. The Pope, by his preaching and miracles, converted a number of the neighbouring population, and in consequence emissaries were sent to put him to death. He was flung into the sea with an anchor attached to his neck. A chapel is said to have been formed by angels' hands, in which the body was found when the sea ebbed,

which annually became accessible on his festival.
His martyrdom took place on the 23rd of November,
in the third year of Trajan.

Clement sent Gratian, Ursinus, and Saturninus
into Gaul, and ordained Eugenius Bishop of Toulouse. He decreed many things with regard to the
sacred vestments and the ornaments of bishops and
archbishops ; he added to the liturgy, and put the
canon in a more exact form ; he appointed notaries,
one for each of the seven regions of the city—which,
as before mentioned, remained out of the fourteen
after the conflagration—to record the acts of the
martyrs ; he held ordinations in the month of
December, which was then the one appointed time,
in which he created fifteen bishops, ten priests, and
two deacons. He was Pope for nine years and two
months.

The mention of these ordinations held by the
Popes leads to the subject of the clergy of Rome
and the cardinals. The word means the principal
or head clergy, and their origin is co-existent with
the Papacy. It was necessary for the Head of the
Church to have coadjutors in a work of such vast
extent. Such were Linus, Cletus, Clement, Anacletus, and Mark, even in the time of St. Peter ;
Linus and Cletus were his bishops, Clement and
Anacletus his deacons. The seven deacons were
appointed to attend to the seven regions, and, of
course, were important persons of the clergy. The
" titles " were churches where the Sacraments were
administered, and where incomes were provided or
houses attached by the gift of pious benefactors, as

that of Pastor or St. Pudentiana, and afterwards of Lucina, Eudoxia, Emiliana, and the rest. To these were appointed cardinal or principal clergy, sometimes more than one over each ; as, for example, to the title of Julius there were three. Pope Evaristus is said to have divided the parishes more exactly, and after him Hyginus. The titles were increased under St. Silvester, when the donations to the churches had increased in number and value. The numbers accordingly varied ; Cletus ordained twenty-five priests, and the most ancient titles were twenty-eight. The cardinals in after times numbered seventy, and Platina says that once, in Paschal II.'s time, there were ninety. It is well to mention this once for all, as the ordinations held by each Pope are always noted, and this is not without its significance.

After the death of Clement, the See was vacant twenty-two days.

CHAPTER III.

A.D. 100.—Anacletus, an Athenian, the son of Antiochus, ordained deacon by St. Peter, succeeded Clement, and was Pope from the second year of Trajan to the eleventh, in the third great persecution. About the time of his accession St. John the Evangelist died. Anacletus has been by some confounded with Cletus, the third Pope; but Cletus was a Roman, Anacletus an Athenian. He made a memorial to his father, Antiochus, and, legislating for the Church, decreed that no prelate or clerk should wear a beard or long hair, that holy orders should be given publicly, and that a bishop should be ordained by three consecrating bishops, a custom established by St. Peter. He also ordained that all present at Mass should communicate or retire. He added the "Dominus vobiscum" and "Pax vobis," though these forms are of more ancient and Eastern origin. He is said also to have written some decretal letters.

Numerous martyrdoms took place in his Pontificate. The most celebrated was that of the great Bishop of Antioch, St. Ignatius. The second Bishop of Antioch was Evodius, ordained by St. Peter, and

Ignatius the third, or, as some say, the coadjutor of
Evodius, ordained by St. Paul bishop of the Gentiles. He was put in chains, to be sent prisoner to
Rome, and ten satellites, or guards, were chained to
him, whom he calls ten leopards. On his way he
wrote epistles to the churches, which contain admirable matter and ardent aspirations for martyrdom. He begs the Christians not to pray that the
beasts may spare him. "I know," he says, "what is
good for me. Come fire, come the cross, come the
breaking of my bones, and the wild beasts, that I
may find Jesus Christ! Welcome the crushing of
my whole body, and all the torments of the devil, if
only I may win Christ! May the teeth of the lions
grind me to meal, that I may be made pure bread of
sacrifice!" He suffered with the same constancy,
rejoicing when he heard the roaring of the beasts of
prey, by whom he was torn in pieces, and only a
portion of his bones remained. These were gathered
up and carried to Antioch, where they were laid
outside of the Daphnian Gate, and afterwards
brought to Rome. The ancient record of his martyrdom calls them more precious than gold, and says
they were visited yearly by the faithful with great
devotion.

St. Simeon, the son of Cleophas, the cousin of
Our Lord, the aged Bishop of Jerusalem, suffered in
this persecution, being a hundred and twenty years
old, so that it is said men marvelled to see the constancy with which a man of so great age endured a
lingering death by crucifixion.

Pliny the younger, governor of a province, moved

to pity by the numbers of Christian martyrs, writes to Trajan, "that multitudes are daily put to death in whom there is no other crime than that they meet together before dawn of day to sing hymns, and that adultery and such other things are forbidden among them." Trajan wrote in reply, "That Christians were not to be hunted out, but if accused, to be punished."

Anacletus assigned sepulchres for the martyrs separate from others. He adorned the sepulchre of St. Peter with a chapel or memorial, as far as could be done with secrecy in such times of persecution. He held one ordination in the month of December, in which he created six bishops, five priests, and three deacons. He was martyred in the eleventh year of Trajan, having sat in the chair of Peter nine years and two months. The See was vacant for thirteen days.

A.D. 110.—Evaristus, the son of Juda, a Bethlemite, succeeded Anacletus. In his time Trajan died of dysentery at Seleucia, in Isauria, having been emperor for eighteen years. He was much lamented by the people, and his body was embalmed and brought to Rome, where it was laid under his beautiful spiral pillar, which is a hundred and forty feet high, adorned with representations in relief of his wars and victories, to be seen in the Foro Traiano. He was munificent in works for the public good, in building bridges over rivers and making roads, and he made the seaport at Ancona. To the deserving he was bountiful in rewards, and so renowned for hospitality, that he was thought to exceed in this. But notwithstanding, the persecution continued to rage in many provincial towns. The history of Faustinus and Jovita, brothers, noblemen of Brescia, recorded on the 15th of January, shows how violent it was in this emperor's time. They were thrown into prison at Brescia, exposed to wild beasts, and put to many torments; then dragged in chains to Milan, where they were again tormented, and from thence sent to Rome as obstinate Christians, where they were comforted and consoled by Pope Evaristus. From Rome they were sent to Naples, and there bound hand and foot and flung into the sea. Preserved miraculously from death, they were sent back to Brescia, and martyred on the accession of Hadrian.

The romantic story of St. Eustace and his family is another instance. He had served Trajan as commander in the Dacian wars, and became a Christian in his residence at Tivoli, being converted by a miracle. A stag brought to bay bore a crucifix between its horns, and a voice addressed him, bidding him to receive baptism and prepare for great sufferings for the faith. He was sentenced to banishment, and the slaves revolted on his estate. Taking passage from Ostia with his wife and children, he was turned adrift on the coast of Africa with his two little sons, the captain of the vessel detaining their mother whom he sold for a slave. In crossing a river, he was robbed of his sons by a lion and a bear. After fifteen years, he was sought for by Trajan, and found labouring on a farm. Restored to his command, he recovered his wife and his lost children, who were brought to his notice by their distinguished valour in battle.   They suffered martyrdom at Rome for refusing to sacrifice to the gods, in the brazen bull, at the accession of Hadrian.

History is silent on topics so disagreeable, and England's Elizabeth is praised while the martyred priests and confessors of the faith are ignored or traduced.   Heathen writers say nothing of Christian malefactors led through the towns of Italy, and Japanese historians will recount as little of the Catholic martyrs led round and exhibited in the cities of Japan.   Of Trajan it was usual to say at the installation of emperors down to the time of Justinian, 'May you be more fortunate than Augustus, more excellent than Trajan."

Evaristus appointed priests to the several titles in the city.   Each title or endowed church had a veil or tabernacle where the Holy Eucharist was reserved. The veil was ornamented with a cross, and, as some suppose, was the origin of the word ciborium, which is thought to be a corruption of siphorium, or the curtain, still retained by the Greeks.   It seems to have represented the mystery of the Holy Eucharist, Christ veiled under the Blessed Sacrament, and the priest going within the veil to have typified the Ascension of the Lord, veiled by a cloud, from the eyes of the beholders.   Evaristus also appointed that the seven deacons should assist the Pope when he preached.   He decreed that laymen should not accuse a bishop. Papias, Bishop of Hierapolis, wrote in his time—a disciple of the priest John, a learned man, whose doctrine was followed by Tertullian and Irenæus ; but it seems he is not to be confounded with St. John the Apostle. Pope Evaristus held three ordinations, and created five bishops of various sees, six priests, and two deacons. He was martyred on the accession of Hadrian, and was buried in the chapel over the tomb of St. Peter, built by Anacletus. He was Pope for nearly ten years. The See was vacant nineteen days.

A.D. 121.—Alexander, the son of Alexander, a Roman of the region Caput Tauri, succeeded to the Pontificate. He was young in years, according to some only twenty, though others say thirty, but was ripe in wisdom, and a great Pope. He is said to have studied under Plutarch and Pliny.

It was an age in which there was an affectation of learning. Ælius Hadrian, the emperor, was learned in both languages, Greek and Latin, and took pleasure in the company of Plutarch and other men of letters. He collected a library at Athens, which he ornamented with buildings, and restored the bridge over the Cephisus. Initiated in the Eleusinian mysteries, he was reputed a favourer of the false gods, and gave occasion to a fanatical outbreak of persecution. But as a philosopher he was, or affected to be, open to remonstrance, and he read an apology for Christianity, presented to him by the bishop Quadratus. Aristides, a Christian scholar, who wore a philosopher's gown, also presented him with a similar work, which induced him to soften in some degree the severities against the Christians, and he wrote to Minucius Fundanus, proconsul of Africa, not to put them to death unless they were proved guilty of some crime. At Rome Hadrian built the

bridge over the Tiber called by his name, and the
Mole of Hadrian for his mausoleum, now called the
Castle of St. Angelo.   In Britain he made a wall
between Solway and Newcastle-upon-Tyne, eighty
miles in length, to keep back the Picts and Scots
from their incursions.   Being a traveller throughout
the world, and an admirer of art, he built at an
enormous expense his curious villa at Tivoli, containing in its vast circuit imitations of many famous
buildings and places, with a miniature Vale of Tempe.
He was also a legislator ; but if we would form a
true idea of Hadrian as an idolater, we must turn to
the acts of St. Symphorosa's martyrdom.   On occasion of the solemn dedication of his villa at Tivoli
he inquired of the gods by sacrifice.   The oracle
replied that the gods were tormented by Symphorosa
and her sons.   That noble lady was summoned before
the emperor, and commanded to do sacrifice.   She
replied : " My husband Getulius and his brother
Amantius, your tribunes, emperor, preferred to die,
beheaded by your command."   Angered at her reply,
Hadrian bade her be beaten with fists in the face,
then she was hung up by her long hair, and finally
flung into the river with a stone about her neck.   Her
seven sons were hauled aloft by pulleys upon seven
platforms, round the temple of Hercules.   The throat
of the eldest, Crescentius, was cut open, the breast
of Julian split asunder, Nemesus was pierced in the
heart, Primitivus in the stomach, Justinus in the
loins, the sides of Stacteus were ripped open, and
Eugenius, the youngest, divided asunder from head
to foot—doubtless, as Röhrbacher observes, in ac-

cordance with superstitious rules of magical art.
Such a scene, suited to the idolatrous savages of
Mexico, needs no comment, but it tells the horrors
of heathen worship.

The youthful and learned Pope made many converts among the Roman nobility. Amongst these
was Hermes, prefect of the city, with his wife
Theodora, and all his household. St. Sabina, a
noble Roman lady, suffered martyrdom, and with
her St. Sapphira of Antioch. Alexander was accused, taken, and brought before the judge Aurelian.
He was racked, torn with hooks, and perforated with
sharp instruments, and finally beheaded, with Eventius, his priest, and Theodulus, his deacon. He
suffered on the 3rd of May, A.D. 131 or 132.

Pope Alexander added the words in the Mass
which precede the Consecration—" Qui pridie quam
pateretur "—in memory of Christ's Passion. He
commanded holy water, blessed with prayers and
mixed with salt, to be kept in churches and private
houses to drive away demons, and decreed that water
should be mixed with the wine at Mass, and that
altar breads should be made of unleavened bread ;
but it is not probable that these things were first
done by him, but were usages from Apostolic time.
In his time the heretic Basilides was confuted by
Agrippa, and joining Bar Cochebas, the false prophet
of the Jews, in his insurrection, perished in it. To
punish the Jews for this rebellion, in which they had
been cruel to the Christians, Hadrian forbade them
to enter Jerusalem, which he rebuilt and called after
his own name—Ælia. He allowed the Christians to

dwell there, and Mark, the first Gentile bishop of Jerusalem, was chosen at that time.

Alexander took refuge in the Catacombs. It is the first mention of these as a hiding-place, and it is evident, from their nature, that they could not have afforded an asylum for many refugees, or that this was the service for which these extraordinary excavations were intended. They were begun and gradually extended for the purposes of Christian burial, and only at times served for the concealment of the more noted victims of persecution, and especially of the Popes. The tomb of Alexander has been discovered in modern researches, which have verified dates and wonderfully confirmed the places of sepulture, and the names of martyrs given in the ancient Martyrologies. The Catacombs are a running comment on the truth of the acts of the martyrs. They are a visible proof opened to us after a lapse of ages, fresh and intact, of the faith, the sacraments, and the worship of the early Christians, and still more of the multitudes who suffered in the persecutions.

St. Jerome attests, in his comments on Ezekiel, that the Catacombs were devoutly visited in the fourth century. In the two following centuries, Celestine I. and John I. adorned with paintings the cemeteries of St. Priscilla, and of St. Nereus and Achilleus. After the inroad of the barbarians, John VII., Gregory III., and Paul I. made some restorations, and recommended these holy places to the veneration of the faithful. In the twelfth century they are mentioned by Peter Mallius, and in the thirteenth as among the "Marvels of the City of Rome." During the absence of the Popes at Avignon they were forgotten. In the time of Sixtus V. attention was called to them by that great Pope. Panvini, and then Bosio, the Oratorian, followed by Aringhi and Boldetti, opened and successively explored this mine of Christian antiquity. Their volumes, filled with illustrations, have fortunately preserved most interesting pictures, now to be no longer seen. Father Marchi and the Chevalier Rossi have continued the work.

The Catacombs may be described as a library in corridors, on whose shelves are deposited as a record the bones of the saintly dead. Except a portion on the Janiculum, they run round the environs of Rome. That on the Janiculum is the most ancient, where St. Peter was entombed. The next is that of Processus and Martinian, the gaolers of the Mamertine, on the Aurelian road. The cemetery of Priscilla is also of an early age, the opening of which, in the time of Baronius, created much admiration, in which the body of St. Pudentiana was laid beside her father on the Salarian road. The family of Pudens consisted of Priscilla, his wife; Pudens, his son; and his children, Timothy and Novatus, Pudentiana and Praxedes. The bodies of St. Pudentiana and Praxedes, with the vases of blood—which they collected with care—of other martyred saints as related in their acts, were found in the time of Paschal I. The short inscriptions of "sweet soul," "dearly beloved," "innocent soul," "most faithful servant of God," and others similar,

so often repeated in the Catacombs, with the un-
mistakable emblems of the dove with the olive
branch, the fish, the anchor, and the palm, suffice to
show that these sepultures are Christian. The
figures of the stag, the lamp, and the bunch of
grapes are less clearly intelligible, unless they are
interpreted by the deep mystical symbolism which
is so frequent in the Catacombs. The early Christians were imbued with the love of parables, or
figures representative of some secret meaning. The
language of the martyrs was often couched in such
expressions. "Now is the time of vintage," said
St. Eugenia, "when the good grapes are gathered
to be pressed." It is the language of the Holy
Spirit, by which the ancient histories of the Old
Testament become intelligible through the New.
Moses striking the rock, giving the living water;
Jonas rising from the mouth of death, represented
by the whale; Noah looking forth from the ark to
receive the olive bough; Daniel among the lions,
are emblems continually repeated, figuring Christ in
His life, death, or resurrection. Sometimes He is
the Good Shepherd, or again is forgiving sins, raising
the paralytic or the dead to life. Again there is the
fish bearing the chalice, or bread touched by a wand
to represent the Holy Eucharist. These are but a
few examples of pictures in the Catacombs, which, in
the language of an old poet, "are speaking to the
wise." Even Orpheus with his lute, charming the
seven beasts, is brought in to typify the power of
Divine grace upon the soul.

The cemetery on the Appian Way, named afterwards from St. Callixtus, existed in the second century, and in it a vast number of martyrs were buried. The bodies successively laid there are numbered at sixty-four thousand, and near to it, on this road, is the pit especially named "Ad Catacumbas," where the bodies of St. Peter and Paul lay for a considerable time, according to the tradition recounted above, and endorsed by St. Gregory, when in the very first age the oriental Christians endeavoured furtively to remove the bodies of the Apostles, whom they claimed as their compatriots, and, frightened by a storm, laid them in this resting-place, which is probably the origin of the word. In the catacomb upon the Appian Way, Pope Urban was concealed when Cecilia sent Valerian to find him.

Father Oldoin relates that Alexander, when put in chains by the judge Aurelian, was miraculously delivered, and, to the astonishment of Aurelian, appeared unfettered before him; also that he was thrown into the fire, from which he came forth unhurt. He held three ordinations in December, creating five bishops, five priests, and three deacons. He was buried at the seventh milestone on the Nomentan Way, where he suffered, having been Pope ten years. The See was then vacant for twenty-five days.

CHAPTER IV.

ST. SIXTUS, ST. TELESPHORUS, ST. HYGINUS, ST. PIUS,
ST. ANICETUS, ST. SOTER.

FOURTH PERSECUTION UNDER THE ANTONINES.

A.D. 132.—Sixtus, the son of Pastor, a Roman of the region Via Lata, succeeded Alexander. At the close of his time Hadrian died, leaving a little poetical melancholy effusion addressed to his parting soul : "O my poor soul, whither art thou going, fleeting and wandering into regions dark and unknown, where thou wilt have thy pleasures no more." He died of a dropsy, or cutaneous disease, in the twenty-second year of his empire, and was succeeded by Antoninus, surnamed the Pious, a native of Cisalpine Gaul.

Pope Sixtus decreed that the holy vessels should not be touched except by those in sacred Orders, and that corporals should be made of the finest linen ; also that bishops visiting Rome should take back with them letters commendatory from the Pope, to show to their people that they were approved by him, or that their cause referred to Rome was decided in their favour. Sixtus added to the Mass the "Sanctus, Sanctus, Sanctus" to be sung at the Preface. For the Mass was at first brief. St.

Peter, when he consecrated, in addition to the form of consecration, used the Lord's Prayer. James, the Bishop of Jerusalem, increased the number and the length of the prayers, and afterwards St. Basil. SS. Linus, Clement, and Alexander, as noted above, added to the canon of the Mass, and put it in more exact form. Celestine afterwards added the Introit; St. Gregory the Kyrie and Gradual; Telesphorus, or Stephen, the Gloria; Gelasius, the Collects. The Epistle and Gospel, if not usual before, were added by Damasus and St. Jerome. The Alleluia was taken from the Church of Jerusalem. The Nicene Creed from or after the Council. Pelagius formulated the Commemoration of the Dead, which was of Apostolic usage; Innocent, the Pax; Sergius, the Agnus Dei. The Confession before the Mass is attributed to Damasus.

Gaul, destitute of bishops, sent to the Pope to petition for aid, and Peregrinus, a Roman, a legate commissioned by Sixtus, having preached the faith, was martyred. The frequent martyrdoms at this time in Gaul are said to have caused this paucity of pastors.

Sixtus held three ordinations in the usual month of December, and created four bishops, eleven priests, and eleven deacons. He suffered martyrdom, according to the Roman Martyrology, under Antoninus Pius, on the 6th of April, A.D. 142, following the chronology of Baronius, and was buried by the tomb of St. Peter, on the Vatican, having been Pope for ten years, three months, and twenty-one days. The See was vacant only two days.

A.D. 142.—Telesphorus, of Thuria, in Calabria, was chosen the ninth Pope. His father became an anchorite, or hermit, or, as some say, Telesphorus himself was an anchorite, for this kind of life was followed in the earliest times of Christianity, and, indeed, before it, by Elias and St. John the Baptist, and the Essenians. At this time the Valentinian heresy arose. These heretics said that Christ took nothing from the substance of the Virgin Mary, but came through her as water passes through a conduit. Justin, the philosopher of the city of Neapolis, in Palestine, wrote against Marcion, who, following Cerdo, maintained that the two principles of mercy and justice in God were antagonistic, and that Christ was not the Son of the Creator Who made the world. He also answered Crescens, the cynic, whom he reproved as a glutton and a sensualist, and afraid to die, and refuted his blasphemies against Christ. Accused by him, he was brought to his death, and suffered martyrdom for the faith. He wrote an " Apology for Christianity," which he presented to the emperors, and a Dialogue with Trypho, the Jew.

The Emperor Antoninus Pius was a promoter of heathen worship and the ancient false religion. He joined his son-in-law Marcus Aurelius, and Lucius Verus with him, as partners in the empire. The character of zeal for religion in the so-called good emperors often fostered an increase of bigotry, and was the cause of more cruel persecution. Marcus Aurelius issued, as we read in Röhrbacher (vol. v. p. 120), the following decree :

" Aurelius, emperor, to all his administrators and

officers,—We have heard that those who call themselves Christians, in these our days, transgress the laws. Apprehend them, and if they refuse to sacrifice to the gods, punish them with torments. Let justice be mingled with severity if on punishment they renounce their crime."

This their crime and transgression of the laws is apparently their refusal to conform with the religion of the false gods. As an example of the decree above, St. Felicitas and her seven sons were summoned to be examined before Publius, the prefect of the city, and the process of their examination taken to Aurelius. They were sentenced to die by torments. The eldest of her sons was beaten to death by whips loaded with balls of lead; the second and third by blows with clubs or bludgeons; the fourth was precipitated headlong, and the three younger children were beheaded. The mother suffered the last.

Pope Telesphorus decreed the fast of the seven weeks of Lent, to be kept in common by all, which had been a traditional observance from Apostolic time, and had partially been neglected. Also that three Masses should be said on Christmas Day—the first at midnight, the second at dawn, the third at break of day. He is said to have added the Gloria in Excelsis to the Mass. He held four ordinations, and created thirteen bishops, fifteen priests, and eight deacons. He was apprehended as an enemy of religion by the false priests of the idols, and was martyred on the 5th of January, A.D. 152, after a Pontificate of eleven years, three months, and twenty-two days, and was buried near St. Peter, on the Vatican. The See was vacant seven days.

A.D. 152.—Hyginus, an Athenian, the son of a philosopher, was the tenth Pope, by whom the gradation of rank in the clergy was more accurately determined, and the parishes or districts of Rome divided under the titular or cardinal priests. To him are attributed decrees on the form of churches, and the consecration of altars with chrism, and on baptisteries ; also that in baptism there should be a godfather and godmother, and that material for church building should not be applied to profane purposes, nor churches be enlarged or diminished without consent of the bishop ; that no metropolitan should condemn a bishop without the consent of the bishops of his province—though this is attributed by some to Pope Pelagius.

The age of the Antonines has been much praised. Antoninus Pius was a liberal benefactor of the people, and assisted with large sums the rebuilding of houses devastated by an inundation of the Tiber. The ports of Terracina and Gaieta were rebuilt and beautified in his time, and a spiral pillar raised either by him or to his memory. In Britain he built the wall or trench which ran between the Firth of Forth and the Clyde ; for, as Camden has shown, the wall of Hadrian was between the Solway and the Tyne ; but in the time of Antoninus, the Scots were driven farther back, and the wall which had been begun by Agricola restored. The wall of Hadrian was again restored by Severus, and fortified with towers at a later period, with a tubular telephone from tower to tower to give signals. But notwithstanding his public benefits, as we have seen, Marcus Aurelius was a persecutor ; Lucius Verus Commodus, his associate in the empire, was an odious prince ; and Commodus, the son of Aurelius, equalled the worst of the preceding emperors in vileness of life and manners. His glory was to exhibit in the arena as a gladiator, or as a Hercules, whose name he assumed, killing beasts in the amphitheatre with a club. The persecution raged in the time of the Antonines, though it culminated in Commodus.

Melito, Bishop of Sardis, wrote a Christian Apology, which he presented to Marcus Aurelius. Tertullian highly praises this work, and calls him a prophet of the Christians. Theophilus of Antioch also wrote against Marcion, and against Hermogenes, who held the first matter to be God.

Hyginus wrote two Epistles, one of which was a general letter to the faithful. He was Pope four years, from the year 152 to 156. He is styled a martyr, and was buried near the body of St. Peter. He held three ordinations in December, and created six bishops, fifteen priests, and five deacons. The See was vacant four days.

A.D. 156.— Pius, the son of Ruffinus, a native of Aquileia, was the eleventh Pope. Lucius Verus died of apoplexy, and Marcus Aurelius became sole emperor. He was an admirer of philosophers, and placed the statue of Fronto, his master, in the senate-house. He was a warlike prince, and, accompanied by his son Commodus in his campaigns, conquered the Marcomanni, Quadi, and Sarmatians. Being in want of money to pay his troops, he sold by auction, in the Forum of Trajan, his furniture and his wife Faustina's jewels, and when he returned victorious, offered the price to the purchasers, though he did not oblige them to give up what they had bought. His liberality in this, and in rewarding his soldiers, as well as in remitting taxes and forgiving debts, publicly burning bonds for money due to the treasury, made this emperor so beloved by the people, that it was counted a sacrilege not to have his image in the house.

St. Pius consecrated the Church of St. Puden-tiana at the request of St. Praxedes, in whose Acts it is mentioned that the Pope buried her father, Pudens the younger, and visited often her sick brother, Novatus. This church was consecrated under the title of Pastor, in her house, near the baths of Novatus, in the Patrician Street; a bap-tistery was made in it, and the whole of the house-hold, ninety-six persons, according to the Roman Bre-viary, May 19th, there received baptism. Pope Pius often said Mass in this church, and adorned it with gifts. Hermas, the brother of the Pope, wrote his book, entitled "The Pastor," in the time of Pius. It contains revelations, similar to those of the Apo-calypse, of great persecutions to ensue; also the command of an angel on the keeping of Easter on the Sunday. A decree to this effect was made by this Pope; also that no one obstinately adhering to the Jewish law should be baptised. He decreed, moreover, penance of forty days for negligence in letting the Sacred Blood fall upon the ground; of three days if it fell on the altar; but if so as to stain the second cloth or linen, of nine days; that the Sacred Blood should, if it were possible, be reverently received by the tongue; but if not, that the spot on which it fell should be washed and scraped, and the purification be thrown into the sacrarium or burned.

In his time, Apollinaris, Bishop of Hierapolis, wrote an Apology, which he presented to Marcus Aurelius. He wrote also against the false prophetesses, Priscilla and Maximilla, the devotees of Montanus, the pretender to the effusion of the Holy Ghost. Tatian, a disciple of St. Justin, wrote at this time, at first well, and afterwards maintaining abstinence, which, carried to further excess by Severus, was called the heresy of the Encratites, against whom Musanus wrote. Philip, Bishop of Crete, wrote also against Cerdo and Marcion. Pope Pius is reckoned among the martyrs, and died on the 25th of June, A.D. 167, having been Pontiff eleven years, four months, and three days, and having held five ordinations, in which he created ten bishops, nineteen priests, and twenty-one deacons. The See was vacant for thirteen days.

A.D. 167.—Anicetus, the son of John, a Syrian, of the town Vicomurcus or Humisias, according to St. Damasus, succeeded St. Pius. It is the opinion of some that he preceded Pius, and there is confusion in the history of this period. Hegesippus, who wrote his "Ecclesiastical History" at this time, in a simple style, beginning from the Passion down to this age, says that he came to Rome in the time

of Anicetus, the tenth after Peter (that is if Linus
and Cletus are omitted), and that he remained to the
time of Eleutherius, who at this period was deacon
of Anicetus.　Hegesippus declaims against the hero-
worship of the heathen, and the honours paid to such
men as Antinous, the favourite of Hadrian.　Marcion came to Rome at this time, according to Irenæus, and St. Polycarp met him there.　Being asked
by Marcion if he knew him, "Yes," he replied, " I
know you, the first-born of the devil."　This holy
bishop converted many of the sect of the Marcionites
and Valentinians, and, returning to his bishopric of
Smyrna, was burned alive, at the age of eighty.
He heard a voice from Heaven encouraging him,
and saying, " Polycarp, be a man !"　He stood, it is
said in his Acts, shining like a bright pillar in the
flames, which arched over him, until he was pierced
with a sword, and his blood gushing out quenched
the fire ; a sweet smell arose from the pyre.

Anicetus renewed the decree that no cleric should
wear long hair ; also the former decree that no
bishop should be consecrated by less than three of
episcopal dignity, which was afterwards made a canon
of the Council of Nice.　That all the bishops of
the province should be present at the consecration
of a metropolitan.　That no bishop should prefer a
charge against his metropolitan except to the primate
or the Apostolic See, which was also confirmed
at the Council of Nice, and by succeeding Popes.
Moreover, that without a special title to it, metro-
politans should not be styled patriarchs or primates,
but archbishops.

Thus we find the Popes issuing decrees affecting the whole Church; such was the decree of Pope Pius with regard to Easter and the Jews, and the letter of St. Clement on the schism to the Corinthians. The decree of the keeping Easter on the Sunday was again enforced by Victor on the Eastern Church, as well as on the West, with a threat of excommunication, and was finally obeyed. St. Polycarp pleaded with Pius or Anicetus the custom of the East, and Polycrates, Bishop of Ephesus, was contumacious to Victor; but the authority of Peter prevailed.

Anicetus held five ordinations in the month of December, and created nine bishops, nineteen priests, and four deacons. He was martyred, and buried in the cemetery upon the Appian Way, afterwards called the Cemetery of Callixtus, where Alexander was also buried; and the fact seems to point out the violence of the persecution, and that he probably suffered martyrdom there. Authors vary in the number of the years of his Pontificate. He died on the 16th of May, A.D. (*circiter*) 175. The See was vacant seventeen days.

A.D. 175.—Soter, the son of Concordius, a native of Fundi, in Campania, succeeded St. Anicetus, as the thirteenth Pope. Commodus, the vile son of Aurelius and Faustina, was emperor, in whose time the miracle took place which gave the name to the Thundering Legion. In his letters to the senate, Commodus confessed that when his army was in want of water, rain fell at the prayers of the Christians, with lightning and thunder, which discomfited the Germans and Sarmatians, and that to this he owed the victory. On his return to Rome, he disgraced himself by his debaucheries, exhibited his feats as a gladiator, and put to death the noblest and best senators of Rome. He changed the name of Rome to Commodiana, and the names of the month of August to Commodus, of September to Herculeus, and the rest to similar titles taken from the amphitheatre, which were abolished as soon as he was dead. He died strangled in the house of the Vestal virgins. To his crimes were attributed the burning of the library and temples on the Capitoline, which were set on fire by lightning. The Temple of Vesta, the palace, and a portion of the city, perished in the conflagration.

St. Soter wrote a decretal letter to the bishops of Italy, requiring a priest who celebrated Mass to be fasting, to have two persons at least present at celebration, and that those present, unless they were under some impediment, should communicate ; that religious women should not be allowed to minister in putting incense into the thurible, or touching the pall or corporal.* He also appointed that marriages should be celebrated with due solemnity before a priest, and not clandestinely, with the approval of parents, and in the presence of bridesmaids ; though by some this is ascribed to Evaristus.

---

* In the Breviary, the Communion of all present at Mass is said to have been decreed by St. Soter with regard to the Mass in "Cænâ Domini," and therefore probably only means to enforce the present usage of the clergy present at that Mass. The present practice of the Church is the safest comment on all matters of ritual in ancient times.

Eusebius writes that Dionysius, Bishop of Corinth, disciple of St. Paul, was living in Soter's time, of such eloquence and learning, that his Epistles were read in the churches. Thedotion, a disciple of Tatian, wrote against the heretic Apelles, who maintained that Christ was only apparently man, not really. This heresy was called that of the Phantasiasts. Clement of Alexandria, the master of Origen, composed philosophical works and a book against the Gentiles. Pinytus of Crete was a man of letters, Oppian a poet, and Herodian a grammarian.

It would be interesting to pursue the question how far the schools of philosophy which flourished at Athens and Alexandria contributed to promote or impede Christianity. All profound study without doubt assists and verifies true religion, while a shallow philosophy accompanies and gives birth to error. Plato shows how ridiculous were the pretensions of the Sophists in his day, and how rare a thing it is in the world to find many, or even a few, capable of grasping scientific truth. It is easy to affect the philosopher's gown, but difficult to understand profoundly and clearly the study of the human mind. Hence the Stoics, the Cynics, the new Platonists, and the would-be philosophers are found among the opponents of Christianity, and a few clever apostates like Porphyrius. Apologists for its truth have been mentioned among the philosophers, such as Justin Martyr, Quadratus Bishop of Athens, and others. The greatest intellects in the world have been both Christians and philosophers.

St. Soter held five ordinations in December, and created eleven bishops, eight priests, and nine deacons. The length of his Pontificate is given by Damasus as nine years; by others, as much less. He died a martyr, April 22nd, A.D. (*circiter*) 182, and was buried in the cemetery of Callixtus, on the Appian Way. The See was vacant one day.

CHAPTER V.

FIFTH PERSECUTION UNDER SEVERUS.

A.D. 182.—The fourteenth Pope was Eleutherius, a Greek of the city of Nicopolis, in Epirus. Letters came to him soon after his election from the martyrs in prison at Lyons, by the hands of Irenæus, the arch-priest, relating their sufferings. Photinus, the aged bishop, bore the kicks and beating of the populace at ninety years of age, and Attalus the red-hot chair, and Blandina was tossed by the bull in the amphitheatre. This, with the burning of St. Polycarp, may be called the episode of the persecution of the Antonines. But in the Pontificate of Eleutherius, excepting this furious outburst in Gaul, the Church had rest and Christianity made progress. At Rome many noble families received and acknowledged the faith. The convert Apollonius, a public orator, suffered death for the faith, for making an oration in praise of Christianity, a thing forbidden by law under pain of death. About the beginning of this Pontificate, Lucius, the son of Coel, a British king, sent two messengers to Rome—Elvan and Medvan, or Medwin—to obtain from the Pope mis-

4

sioners to instruct his people in Christianity. Fugatius, or Faganus, and Damianus, or Divianus, Roman priests of learning and dignity, were sent as legates. By them the king and his household were instructed and received the faith, and it is said that instead of the three arch-flamens—so they are called by Ptolemy—three archbishops were appointed at London, Caerleon, and York, with ten bishops in each of their provinces.

It has been objected to this—though the fact is recorded by St. Bede—that the title of a king of Britain is absurd. But, as Alford shows, the line of British kings existed under the Romans, and they maintained their rank in many instances as tributaries, nor was this unusual in the Roman empire. Coel, in particular, the father of Lucius, or Lever Mawr—which means the "great light"—was in favour with the Roman authorities, having served under Titus and Vespasian with the rank of tribune. It is therefore more probable that he would be left in possession of his hereditary right of leader of the British princes, as son of Marius. Christianity had long found a home in Britain before the time of Lucius, and the two messengers to Rome are said to have been Christian cœnobites; nor is the reception of Christianity and destruction of the Druidical superstition in Britain at this time so improbable as it may seem at first sight. There was a line of bishops of London from Theanus, in the time of Lucius, to Theonus, or Theonius, the last who was expelled or martyred by the Saxons when they became masters of the island. The authenticity of the letter of the Pope to Lucius may not bear criticism, but that in the time of Eleutherius, Britain, by his authority, and by commission of learned Roman priests—who in after times would be called cardinal legates—received a hierarchy as a Christian country, cannot be well disputed.

St. Eleutherius decreed against the Encratites that no one should refuse any kind of usual food on account of superstition ; that accusations should not be received against the absent ; that no one should be degraded from his rank in the Church, unless convicted of some crime, after the example of Christ, who bore with Judas as an apostle until he openly prevaricated.

Various sects sprang up out of the heresy of the Marcionites. Some maintained one principle as the cause of sin and evil as well as of good ; others two, antagonistic to each other, and some three principles with three natures, and rejected the ancient prophets. Florinus and Blasco held that God was the author of sin, against whom the Quolitians contended that God was not the author or creator of evil. Modestus wrote against the Marcionites, and Bardesanes, who had been a Valentinian, against the Valentinians. St. Jerome praises him, saying that " If he was so excellent a writer in Greek, what must he have been in his native Syriac ?" Galen, the great physician, whose life was a long one, and extended over a considerable period, is placed by some at this time.

After the death of Commodus, Pertinax, prefect of the city, was chosen by the senate, and made emperor, against his will, at the age of seventy. He refused the title of Augusta for his wife and of Cæsar for his son, to show that the imperial dignity was forced upon him. Pertinax was niggardly in his habits, and soon incurred the hatred of the rapacious Prætorian Guard, by whom the empire was put up to the highest bidder, and bought by Didius Julianus, a lawyer, at the price of an immense donative or largess to the soldiers, and Pertinax was murdered by them in his palace.

Eleutherius held three ordinations in December, in which he created fifteen bishops, twelve priests, and eight deacons. He died on the 26th of May, after a Pontificate of thirteen years, or, according to Baronius, of fifteen, and was buried in the Vatican, by the sepulchre of St. Peter. He is styled a martyr, though it is not certain that he died by violence, for this title is given to those who endured persecution for the confession of the faith. The See was vacant five days.

A.D. 195.—Victor, the son of Felix, an African, succeeded Eleutherius, and was the fifteenth Pope. He is reckoned by St. Jerome among the ecclesiastical writers, and it may be observed that at this time three conspicuous figures of the age were Africans. Severus was emperor, an African of the town of Leptis ; Tertullian, the great controversialist, was an African, the son of a centurion of Carthage ; and Victor was Pope.

Didius Julianus was put to death by Severus, after an empire of seven months. Severus was a stern soldier, and cashiered the Prætorian Guard for the murder of Pertinax. He conquered Pescennius Niger, his opponent in the East, and as victor of the Parthians, Adiabenians, and Arabs, is inscribed on his triumphal arch beneath the capitol, Parthicus, Arabicus, Adiabenicus. He made Central Arabia a Roman province, and in Rome built the baths of Severus between the Palatine and Cælian. Nor was he unacquainted with letters, but was studious of philosophy. According to Tertullian, he was not unfavourable to Christians until he was urged to persecute by the cruelty of Plautianus Lateranus, his father-in-law, and at his instigation the fifth violent persecution began under Severus.

In the fifth year of Pope Victor and the fourth of Severus, the controversy which had been moved in the time of Pope Pius on the celebration of Easter, revived. The Asiatic bishops were accustomed to end the fast of Lent and begin Easter-time on the fourteenth day of the moon in March, after the vernal equinox, on whatever day of the week it fell. This custom was not universal in the East, and in the West the custom was to keep Easter on the Sunday next after the fourteenth day of the moon, by Apostolical tradition. Pope Pius, and, according to Damasus, Pope Eleutherius, had passed a decree that the Apostolical tradition should be observed, and that Easter should not be kept at the same time with the Jewish Pasch. Victor, summoning a council of bishops—one of whom, Theophilus of Cesarea, was a skilful mathematician—passed a decree to the effect of keeping Easter on the Sunday, and drew up a Paschal Cycle for the observance of it.

Polycrates, the Bishop of Ephesus, refused obedience to this decree, maintaining the Asiatic custom, saying that he followed the authority of the ancients and of the Apostle St. John. "We," he said, "keep the very day on which it fell, neither adding nor diminishing; this opinion St. Philip followed, who died at Hierapolis, and St. John, who leaned upon the bosom of the Lord. . . . Polycarp and Thraseas, Melito and Narcissus, Bishop of Jerusalem, did the same." Councils held at Cesarea by Theophilus, in Gaul by Irenæus, in Corinth by Bacchylus, in Pontus, Tyre, and Jerusalem, received the decree and assented to it; but Polycrates remained obstinate, with a number of Asiatic bishops. The Pope insisted, and would have excommunicated them, but was persuaded by St. Irenæus to relax. Afterwards the decree of Victor was made a canon of the Council of Nice. Victor also decreed that baptism should be generally given at Easter-time, but in case of necessity at any time, and that then common water could be used. Also he forbid the accusation of bishops without manifest evidence, and that their causes should be referred to the Apostolic See.

This learned and energetic Pope excommunicated Theodotus of Byzantium, the tanner of Corinth, who denied the Divinity of Christ, and Praxeas, the Patripassian. In his time Appion wrote his Hexaemeron, and Sextus on the Resurrection. Arabianus wrote a summary of Christian doctrine, and Judas a history of Christianity down to the tenth year of Severus, in which he held an erroneous opinion of the immediate coming of Antichrist, be-

cause it appeared to him that the cruelty and
wickedness of the world had reached such a pitch,
that God could endure it no longer. St. Victor is
styled a martyr, and was buried near St. Peter on
the Vatican on the 26th of July. He was Pope for
ten years and three months. The See was vacant
twelve days.

A.D. 205.—Zephyrinus, a Roman, the son of
Abundius, succeeded Victor and was the sixteenth
Pope. In the second year of his Pontificate the
persecution began to rage in the East in which
Leonides, the father of Origen, was martyred. St.
Perpetua and Felicitas suffered in Africa, and their
history is one of the most beautiful of the touching
acts of the martyrs. The vision of St. Perpetua, in
which she saw a ladder to heaven, beneath which
lay an ugly monster, on whose head she first set her
foot, and then scaled the stairs with ease, illustrates
the painful sacrifices in private life which must have
so frequently accompanied martyrdom. This previous
conflict signified in the vision was the encounter with
the tears and reproaches of her aged heathen father,
who besought her not to load her family with dis-
grace, and bring down his grey hairs with sorrow to
the grave. St. Martina in Rome was an example of
heroic protracted endurance, and her martyrdom,
signalised by stupendous miracles, is kept on the
30th of January. Revocatus, Saturninus, Pammachius, Calepodius, and Quirinus, are some of the
names of suffering saints in this persecution; and at
Lyons, St. Irenæus closed a holy life with a martyr's
death.

Pope Zephyrinus decreed that priests and deacons should be ordained publicly in the presence of clergy and laity, which was afterwards confirmed in the Council of Chalcedon. Also that the Precious Blood should not be consecrated in wooden chalices, but in glass or crystal. Glass was afterwards forbidden as liable to be broken, and brass or bronze, on account of the taste; gold, silver, and tin were only allowed to be used. The decree is also attributed to him of the injunction of Easter Communion on all Christians past the age of childhood, to which Innocent III. added confession of sins. Also that the presbytery should assist at the bishop's Mass, which had been already decreed by Evaristus.

In the time of Zephyrinus, Heraclitus wrote commentaries on St. Paul, and Candidus composed his Hexaemeron, while the celebrated Origen, after the martyrdom of his father, kept a grammar school to support his widowed mother and her six children. After this he gave himself wholly to religious teaching and preaching, and had disciples martyrs. The heroic Potamiena, led by his precept and example, endured martyrdom by boiling pitch poured upon her head. He went barefoot in practice of consummate poverty, and his abstinence was excessive. He knew all languages and was versed in all kinds of literature, but this wonderful man, by his act of indiscretion in mutilating himself, has left a blot upon his character, and his treatise on "First Principles" has given rise to heresies.

Tertullian was more unfortunate. His stern asceticism led him into heresy and fanaticism, and

his intolerant spirit to impiety and scoffing at the
Pope.   A great head is more dangerous than a great
heart, and while we lament the fall of Tertullian,
the generosity of Origen enlists our sympathy to
hope that his reputed errors have been exaggerated
and his speculations misunderstood.

The Pontificate of Zephyrinus, according to
Baronius and others, was a long one.   Severus died
at York broken-hearted at the parricidal attempts of
Caracalla, his murderous son, who tried to kill his
father, and, it is said, slew his brother Geta in his
mother's arms.   This monster succeeded to the
empire, and, taking the name of Antoninus, completed the Baths called the Antonine and paved the
Via Nova.   It is to be remarked that the great
public baths, which were such a boon to the people
and built with such luxurious magnificence, were
the works of the worst of the emperors in the most
persecuting times, and their stones were cemented
with the sweat and blood of Christians condemned
to slavery.   The baths and the amphitheatres fed
the two favourite sins of the populace of Rome—
lust and the love of bloodshed.   Caracalla died,
assassinated between Carræ and Edessa, and was
succeeded by a boy born at Emesa, reputed to be a
son of Caracalla, but by his mother's side of the
royal Phœnician race of the Priests of the Sun.
Macrinus, who had been chosen by his soldiers to
succeed Caracalla, was soon after slain at Chalcedon,
and Heliogabalus, the boy priest, entered Rome
leading the Chariot of the Sun.   He appointed his
mother and the women of his court to hold the

senate, and amused himself with blowing up with
inflated bellows suddenly expanded, the guests as
they were seated at his table.   He exhibited in the
amphitheatre a hunt of ten thousand mice by a
thousand weasels.   He was flung into the Tiber
with his mother by the Prætorian Guard, after a
disgraceful empire of three years, and was succeeded
by Diadumenus and Albinus, and then by Alexander.

In the second year of Heliogabalus, Pope Zephyrinus died, as some suppose, a martyr for refusing to
sacrifice to the Sun, and was buried " ad Catacumbas,"
near the Cemetery of Callixtus on the Appian Way.
The catacomb in which he was laid is named from
him the Cemetery of Zephyrinus, as it was excavated
by him.   He held four ordinations in December, and
created thirteen bishops, thirteen priests, and seven
deacons.   St. Damasus gives him only eight years,
but Baronius and others eighteen, of Pontificate.   His
memory is kept on the 26th of August.   The See
was vacant six days.

A.D. 221.—St. Callixtus, the son of Domitius, a
Roman, succeeded Zephyrinus, a holy and great
Pope, whose reputation was slandered by a Novatian
heretic.   He had been chained as a slave to work in
the mines of Elva, and a calumny on this account,
which was indeed an honour, and for the misuse of
ecclesiastical revenues, was raised against him.   He
worked miracles, curing Privatus, a leper, and Blanda,
a paralytic.   An energumen seized by the devil cried
out on the Capitol, " The God of Callixtus is the one
true God."   An ancient author of the Lives of the
Popes writes that he built the church of the Blessed

Virgin Sta. Maria in Trastevere, which was the first
public place of worship in Rome, and the site was
obtained by a rescript of the Emperor Alexander,
against the suit of some tavern-keepers who wished
to build cook-shops on the locality. It was the spot
from which the fountain of oil flowed into the Tiber
at the time of the Nativity. It is recorded by St.
Damasus and Lampridius that Callixtus built it,
but whether it was the present ample structure may
be doubted. The expenses of the suit and the
building may have given rise to the accusation
against the Pope of the misuse of funds by the
anonymous author of a libel entitled the "Philoso-
phumena," whose calumnies contributed to bring the
Pontiff to a cruel martyrdom.

Callixtus decreed the fasts of the Quatuor tempora
in which ordinations could be held, hitherto usual in
the month of December only. Also that the accusations of infamous persons should not be received
against the clergy. He condemned the doctrine
that a cleric who had fallen, and done canonical
penance, could not be restored to his dignity, for the
severe dogmas of Novatus began to be prevalent.
Tertullian had given a handle in Africa to the error
of the second baptism of heretics in the time of Pope
Zephyrinus, and now wrote his rigid treatises on
fasting, chastity, and marriage but once allowable.
His school had been frequented by St. Cyprian, who,
as related by St. Jerome, never failed to attend his
lectures daily.

Origen wrote about this time his books against
the Ebionites, the Valentinians, and the apostate

infidel Porphyrius. That acute opponent of Christianity allows him to be the prince of philosophers, and St. Jerome says that his books amounted to six thousand volumes. Alexander, the young emperor who soon succeeded Heliogabalus, was a youth of sixteen, and his mother Mammea sent for Origen from Antioch to come to Rome and instruct her in the Christian religion. Alexander himself is said by some to have been a Christian, but this seems more than doubtful. He was rather a hero-worshipper than a Christian, and had an image of Christ, Abraham, and Orpheus among his domestic gods. It is said that he thought of building a temple to Christ, and he was imbued with many Christian sentiments which were learned perhaps from his mother. One of his sayings was, " Do to others as you would be done by ;" and this he had put up as an inscription in the Forum. His tutor or preceptor was Ulpian the lawyer, an enemy of orthodox Christians, to whom the government of Rome was committed in the absence of Alexander, and he continued the persecution.

Pope Callixtus was accused before Ulpian, and, as it seems, calumniated by the heretics. He was cast into prison, deprived of food, daily beaten with rods, then flung from a window to the ground and finally precipitated into a well. He was the seventeenth Pope, and held five ordinations in the month of December, creating eight bishops, sixteen priests, and four deacons. He was buried in the Cemetery of Calepodius, on the Aurelian Way, on the 14th of October. This cemetery had been made or adorned by St. Callixtus to receive the body of the martyr Calepodius drawn out of the Tiber, and he himself was laid there. The great Cemetery of St. Callixtus is named after him on the Appian Way because it was repaired or beautified by him, or probably greatly extended by the excavators in his time. He was Pope for six years and ten months. The well into which he was thrown is in the church of Sta. Maria in Trastevere. After his death the See was vacant six days.

CHAPTER VI.

A.D. 227.—St. Urban, a Roman, the son of Pontian, was the eighteenth Pope. According to an ancient document he was seven times accused before the judges; and during the whole of his Pontificate was in trouble and persecution. He took refuge in the Catacombs on the Appian Way. There he baptised Valerian and Tiburtius, sent to him by St. Cecilia. They were converted by the sight of the Angel who attended her. She died in her father's house, which, at her request, was dedicated as a church, having endured first the fire of the hypocaust or bath heated to the full, and afterwards remaining three days alive with her head half severed by the stroke of the soldier sent to despatch her, from which he desisted after inflicting three blows with the axe. Urban made many converts, and amongst them Maximus, the chamberlain of the emperor. He made a decree that property given in alms to the Church should be equally divided among the clergy. He commanded plate, for the use of the altar, to be of silver.

Minutius Felix, a Roman pleader of celebrity,

wrote in his time a dialogue between a Christian and a heathen. In this we have recorded the horrible accusations commonly made and received among the heathen against the Christians. Such, for instance, as the worship of an ass's head, the murdering of a child, which was covered with dough or paste, and then eaten; the meeting together in subterranean darkened rooms where the lights were extinguished and every wickedness practised, and other tales too shameful or revolting to be mentioned, forged or imagined at the suggestion of the devil to prevent converts from joining the faith or to cause persecution. Some of these charges originated from the crimes of heretics, and some seem to have been actually alleged by them against Catholics. Minutius Felix also wrote against diviners and astrologers. Alexander, Bishop of Jerusalem, collected a famous library, and Trypho attended the school of Origen.

After a Pontificate of four, or as some say of six years, St. Urban was accused before Ulpian, and condemned. He suffered martyrdom, and was buried in the Cemetery of Prætextatus on the Tiburtine Way. The body was afterwards removed by Pope Paschal to the church of St. Cecilia, when the touching discovery of her remains was made in re building her church in the Trastevere. Urban held ordinations in December, in which he created nine bishops, nine priests, and five deacons. The See was vacant for thirty days.

A.D. 233.—The nineteenth Pope was Pontian, by birth a Roman, the son of Calphurnius. His zeal

for the faith or success in promoting it, awakened
the fury of the priests of the false gods—by whom
he was accused to Alexander, or more probably to
Ulpian.   Alexander was often absent from Rome,
and fought with success against the Persians or
Parthians in the East.   He seems at this time to
have been with his army in the West, for he was
soon afterwards slain in a mutiny of his soldiers at
Mayence on the Rhine.   He was a disciplinarian,
and had disbanded some whole legions for miscon-
duct.   He seems to have been indifferent to the fate
of the Popes, or left the whole matter to Ulpian, by
whom Callixtus, as we have seen, was cruelly martyred, Urban condemned, and Pontian, with his
attendant priests Philip and Hippolytus, was
banished to Sardinia.   There he was kept prisoner,
watched by soldiers, to the time of Maximin, by
whose command he is said to have been beaten to
death with clubs.   Whatever may have been the
faults of Alexander, he was an accomplished prince,
and, with the assistance of Julius Frontinus and
Ulpian the lawyer, endeavoured to amend the state
of Rome politically, to restrain the excesses of the
soldiery, and promote taste for the fine arts.   His
sins against religion were soon thrown into the shade
by Maximin.

The emperors, in proportion to their wickedness,
and sometimes to their profession of philosophy, were
enemies of Christianity, and especially of the Popes.
We now come to some hideous characters who, in accordance with their brutality, endeavoured with the
fury of a wild beast to stamp out the Papacy.   Of this

Maximin, who now appears upon the stage, was a perfect specimen. He was born in Thrace, famous for its athletes, of a Getan or Gothic father and an Alan mother, and was first a herdsman and then a soldier. In stature he exceeded eight feet, drank an amphora at a meal, and consumed, it is said, forty pounds of meat a day. His feet were so large as to become a proverb, and he used his wife's armlet for a ring to his finger. He was chosen emperor by the soldiers without the authority of the senate, and was a fitting character to carry out the unrelenting persecution of the Christians, which he continued during the three years of his reign. Learning was his abomination, and he sought out for destruction the most learned and the best. St. Pontian, according to some, was by his command beaten to death with clubs; others say that he died from the hard treatment he received in his place of exile and death in Sardinia, where his body lay for three years, and was afterwards removed to Rome by Pope Fabian with much solemnity, and buried on the Appian Way near the Cemetery of Callixtus, in the catacomb which took his name. He held two ordinations in the month of December, creating six bishops, six priests, and five deacons, and was Pope for five years. His memory is kept on the 19th of November. The See was vacant for ten days.

A.D. 238.—Antherus the son of Romulus, a Calabrian, was chosen to succeed St. Pontian. According to some authors he was a Calaritan of the Isle of Sardinia, where he was elected Pope, and immediately proceeded to Rome, to console the Christians suffering under the persecution of Maximin. He was careful in commanding the notaries to take down accounts of the acts of the martyrs in the seven regions of the city, an office which had been instituted by St. Clement, and was continued by St. Fabian, the successor of Antherus, who appointed seven sub-deacons to preside over it. The persecution was very violent, and the new Pope was soon taken and brought before Sabinus, the prefect of the city, by Vitalian, the captain of the Prætorian Guard. He was tortured and then beheaded on the 7th of January, so that some give him only one month and a few days of Pontificate ; but according to others he was Pope part of two years, and wrote a decretal letter to the bishops of Spain that " No bishop should be translated from his See for pecuniary advantage, but for the good of the flock committed to him, with the consent of the Apostolic See." This decree, dated in July, would prove, says Father Oldoin, that he was Pope for more than a year. He held only one ordination in December at Fundi in Campania on his way to Rome, in which he created one bishop. He was the twentieth Pope, and was buried in the Cemetery of Callixtus on the Appian Way.

A.D. 240.—For thirteen days the clergy and their persecuted flock hesitated whom to choose. A white dove descended upon Fabian, and he was elected Pope. Fabian the son of Fabius, a noble Roman of the region of the Cœlian Mount, the twenty-first Pope, was diligent in collecting the acts of the martyrs by notaries ; he repaired and beautified the cemeteries, and decreed that the holy chrism should

be every year consecrated on Maundy Thursday,
and the remainder of the last year's chrism be consumed by fire. Also that it should be composed of
balsam mingled with oil. He affirmed that the
solemn consecration of it in Cœna Domini is of
Apostolical tradition.

Maximin besieging Aquileia was slain in his tent
by his soldiers, together with his son. The senate
declared him an enemy of the Roman people, and
the persecutors of the Christians, Sabinus, prefect
of the city, and Vitalian, prefect of the Prætorian
Guard, were both put to death. Gordian was made
emperor; the sixth great persecution ended, and
there was a respite for a time. Gordian, victorious
over the Parthians, was assassinated by Philip, an
Arab chief, and by this crime Philip and his son
Philip succeeded to the empire. They were Christians, or,'as some say, were converted by St. Fabian,
who subjected the emperor to canonical penance for
his sin before he admitted him to the sacraments.

When the new emperors came to Rome from the
East, a thousand years were completed since the
foundation of the city, and the secular games, celebrated every hundred years, were kept with extraordinary magnificence. It was a new epoch, inaugurated by the first promise of the dawn which was
to break upon the world in another half century, and
a beginning of the change which was coming on the
great city when it would pass from its pagan deities
to become the centre of the Catholic Church, no
longer oppressed and persecuted, but reigning under
its head, the Vicar of Christ, dominant over converted

·nations to the end of time.   Rome is linked with the
Papacy, and the Papacy with Rome.   The See is the
bride of Peter until the world falls.   But the time
had not yet come for the freedom of the Church ;
seas of blood were yet to be shed before its deliverance from pagan thraldom.

In the fifth year of his empire, though some give
him seven years, and the second after the celebration
of the anniversary of a thousand years of Rome,
Philip the father was murdered at Verona by the
arts of Decius, and his son Philip at Rome.   The
hatred of Christianity increased in virulence ; and as
Maximin had sought the death of Mammea and her
preceptor Origen, so Decius, following in his steps,
sought the death of Christians as adherents of Philip,
and by cutting off the principal men who professed
it, resolved to exterminate the faith.

In the five or seven comparatively peaceful years
of the time of Philip, St. Fabian adorned the tombs
of the martyrs in the cemeteries, and held a council
at Rome against Novatian the heretic, who denied
that those who had once fallen from the faith could
be restored.   Sixty bishops were assembled, and this
false doctrine was condemned, and it was declared
that no one was incapable of the pardon of his sins.
Origen sent his profession of faith to the Pope, ex-
cusing himself of the charge of heresy, and wrote a
letter of instruction or advice to Philip the emperor
and his wife Severa.   He confuted the heresy that
the soul dies or sleeps with the body until the time
of the resurrection, and then is resuscitated with it ;
and the heresy of the Helcesites who rejected St.

Paul, and maintained that it was no sin to deny
Christ in torments if the faith was retained in the
mind.

He wrote also against Celsus, and it is said
of this indefatigable man that he kept seven writers
employed while he dictated to them. In Africa St.
Cyprian, a noble senator and rhetorician, converted
to the faith by Cœcilius, took his name. The
patriarch of Jerusalem, the aged Narcissus, by his
urgent entreaty compelled Alexander, Bishop of
Cappadocia, who came to visit the holy places, to
take upon him the administration of the patriarchate,
which he fulfilled, until he was taken to Cesarea to
suffer martyrdom in the persecution of Decius, when
the great martyr, St. Babylas, suffered also at
Antioch.

St. Fabian held the Pontificate thirteen or fifteen
years, according as the time of Pope Antherus is
reckoned at two years or a month. He was taken
and put to death at the accession of Decius, and
many of the principal clergy were seized and put in
prison, among whom were Moses and Maximus,
priests, and Nicostratus, deacon, to whom St.
Cyprian wrote in their captivity while the See was
vacant.

It remained vacant for the unexampled space
of a year according to Ciaconius, for the number
of the clergy of Rome was so diminished or dispersed
that they abstained from electing a Pontiff. St.
Fabian held five ordinations, in which he created
eleven bishops, twenty-two priests, and seven deacons.
His feast is kept on the 20th of January with that

of St. Sebastian, but according to an ancient martyrology he suffered on the 20th of March. He was buried in the cemetery of St. Callixtus on the Appian Way; but according to Ferrari a portion of his relics—his head and arm—were venerated at the catacomb of St. Sebastian.

CHAPTER VII.

SEVENTH PERSECUTION UNDER DECIUS.
EIGHTH PERSECUTION UNDER VALERIAN.

A.D. 254.—Cornelius, a Roman of that same noble family, the son of Castinus, was chosen Pope in the place of St. Fabian, and destined to almost certain martyrdom. Decius pretended to reform the abuses under the reign of the Philips, and to put down the Christians as their abettors, and subverters of the imperial majesty of Rome. He was a native of Buda in Hungary, and was declared emperor by the soldiers in Pannonia, over whom he was appointed by Philip. He created his son Decius Etruscus, Cæsar, and as soon as he came to Rome published a bloody edict against the Christians, which he sent into all the provinces, commanding the magistrates to search for them and employ every torment to bring them to submission. The seventh great persecution began with an array of all instruments of torture : fire, the sword, the rack, hooks for tearing the flesh, red-hot plates and bars, and the beasts of the amphitheatre. The saints suffered in great number both in Rome and the provinces. Tryphon and Respicius the tribune were beaten to death with loaded whips after other torments, the feet of Tryphon being transfixed with red-hot nails ; a virgin named Nympha suffered with them. Abdon and Sennen, Persians, accused of burying the bodies of martyred Christians, brought in chains to Rome by command of Decius, were thrown to lions and bears, and when the beasts refused to touch them were beheaded. In Sicily the prætor Quintianus cruelly cut off the breasts of the virgin St. Agatha, who was miraculously cured of her wounds by St. Peter appearing to her in prison, and then suffered martyrdom. At Camerino the boy Venantius, fifteen years of age, endured with sweetness a long conflict. His mouth was beaten in and jaws broken, and he was suspended head downwards over a fire, then thrown to lions who licked his feet, flung from a precipice, and dragged through thorns and briars until the soldiers were weary. Kneeling upon a stone which, as if softer than his persecutors, retained the impression of his knees, he prayed for his murderers, and gave them drink in their thirst by a miraculous spring. Many converts were made by his constancy and miracles, who were beheaded with him. In Alexandria there was a general panic, and St. Apollonia, whose teeth were first struck out, threw herself of her own accord into the flames. At Carthage many fell away for fear. At Antioch St. Babylas died in his prison. St. Paul, the first hermit during the rage of this persecution, retired at the age of fifteen into the desert of the Thebais, and dwelling in a cave clothed in matting of palm leaves, lived a solitary to the age of a hundred and ten, down to the time of Constantine.

In the midst of this persecution, St. Cornelius, a holy priest of the Roman Church, who had regularly ascended the usual degrees of ordination, was elected Pope against his will. St. Cyprian, who received information of the regular and canonical election of Cornelius, has left a record in his letter to Antonianus of the method of a pope's election. By Apostolic usage, some sign was looked for as indicating the person to be chosen. After this the cardinal clergy of the Church of Rome, were assembled and their votes taken one by one. If any foreign bishops were present at the time in Rome, their votes were taken also. Sixteen bishops were present at the election of Cornelius, two of whom, Stephen and Pompeius, were delegates from Africa. From them St. Cyprian had information of the truth which the heresiarch Novatian endeavoured to falsify. The attempt of Novatian to set himself up against Cornelius is the first example of an Antipapal schism. Supported by Novatus from Africa, he obtained some votes of the clergy and of some bishops in Italy to dispute the election of Cornelius, whom he accused of laxity in admitting the lapsed to repentance.

The Emperor Decius was summoned to the frontier to repel the Scythians of the Tanais, and there was betrayed by Gallus, being led into a swamp where he was swallowed up together with his horse, and his body was never found. Gallus succeeded him with his son Volusian. The Christians considered the death of Decius a judgment of God, and there was some little respite from persecution. But the newly-elected Pope was informed against, it seems by the Novatian heretics, and ordered to go into banishment from Rome to Centum Cellæ, now Civita Vecchia, and there neither to write nor receive letters.   It is said by some that before he left Rome he removed the bodies of St. Peter and St. Paul from the cemetery " ad Catacumbas," where they had been thrown in the attempt to carry them to the East, as they were considered no longer safe in that locality, and that he placed the body of St. Paul on the Ostian Way near the spot of his martyrdom, and the body of St. Peter at Montorio.   This is said to have been at the request of the lady Lucina, afterwards conspicuous in her services to the Popes ; but though she lived long and was nineteen years a widow after her husband's death, she was probably too young at this time, and the removal of the bodies was perhaps made at a later period.

St. Cyprian wrote letters to Cornelius at Centum Cellæ, and Cornelius replied.   Information was given to the emperor, and the Pope was summoned to Rome, and according to the acts, brought before the presence of Volusian, who thus addressed him :

" Are you so obstinate a traitor as to contemn the divinities and disobey your emperor by writing and receiving treasonable letters ?"

To which the Pope replied :

" It is no treason to write and receive letters which do not concern the state, but are wholly on spiritual matters and the praises of Christ."

Enraged at this reply, the emperor commanded him to be beaten with loaded whips weighted with balls of lead, and taken to the Temple of Mars to adore his statue. Cornelius, refusing to adore, was beheaded, having first recommended the care of the treasures of the Church to the archdeacon Stephen. He was martyred on the 16th of September, on the same day but not in the same year as St. Cyprian, who suffered several years afterwards. Twenty martyrs were put to death with him, one of whom was Cerealis, a soldier whose wife Sallustia the Pope cured, by a miracle, of paralysis, and converted, and she suffered at the same time. The martyrdom of Cornelius is recorded by St. Damasus. He held the Pontificate two years or part of three, and created, according to some, in two ordinations held in December seven bishops, four priests, and four deacons. According to others he held no ordinations on account of persecution. The lady Lucina is said to have obtained possession of the body of the Pope by night, and of the martyrs who suffered with him ; and, accompanied by the clergy and attendants, to have buried them in her estate near the Cemetery of Callixtus on the Appian Way. The discovery of his sepulchre in modern times on that spot, is given in Dr. Northcote's interesting book on the Catacombs. The See was vacant after his death for a month and five days.

St. Cornelius held a council in Rome, at which sixty bishops were present and a greater number of priests and deacons, in which he condemned the cruel doctrine of the Novatians, and confirmed the decrees of the first council of Carthage, held by St. Cyprian on the reception of the fallen to penitence.

A.D. 255.—Lucius the son of Porphyrius, a priest

of Rome who had been companion of Cornelius in
exile, was elected to succeed him, and was almost
immediately ordered into banishment, upon which
St. Cyprian wrote to congratulate him on the double
honour of being pontiff and confessor. His exile was
not long, and again St. Cyprian wrote to wish him
joy on his return. The cause of this permission to
return was the death of Gallus and Volusian, slain
by their own soldiers as they marched against
Emilian, the leader of the Pannonian legions ; and
he, after a short reign of three months, was put to
death, and Valerian, the commander of the German
legions, declared emperor with his son Licinius Gallienus, whom the senate created Cæsar.

The Tiber overflowed its banks and inundated the
city. A fearful pestilence raged throughout the
world, leaving neither province nor people and
scarcely a family untouched. The nations of the
north began to threaten and hang like a thunder-
cloud on the horizon. Valerian at first seemed mild
and favourable, but became for three years and a
half a most dreadful persecutor, so as to be thought
the true Antichrist, until he met with a fearful retribution, taken captive in Persia.

St. Lucius, the twenty-third Pope, decreed that
two priests and three deacons should accompany the
Pontiff to be witnesses of his life and conversation,
which seems to have been a precaution taken against
the false accusations of the Novatian heretics. According to some, the council against them was held
by Lucius. Origen died about the beginning of his
Pontificate, aged sixty-nine, in the city of Tyre.

One of his last works was against Celsus the Epicurean. The cruel prefect of Rome, Perennius, the instrument of Valerian, inaugurated the persecution by the execution of the Pope. He was beheaded, and on his way to death committed the care of the Church a second time to Stephen the archdeacon, as Cornelius had done before him. He was Pope for about two years, and created in two ordinations held in December, seven bishops, four priests, and four deacons. He was buried in the Cemetery of Callixtus on the Appian Way. The See was vacant a month and five days.

A.D. 258.—St. Stephen the son of Julius, a Roman and archdeacon of the Holy Roman Church, was elected twenty-fourth Pope. Letters passed between him and St. Cyprian on the baptism of heretics. The Pope enforced the Apostolical tradition that baptism administered in proper form is valid, and not to be repeated. The Montanists and Donatists re-baptised Catholics who fell away to them, and Tertullian is said to have given countenance to this practice. Rome launched its sentence against it, and the bishops of the Synod of Iconium were excommunicated by Stephen for adhering to it. The bishop of Alexandria, the learned Dionysius, was brought to submission and agreement with the Pope, and he wrote to say that the bishops of Asia and Africa had now come to the same mind. Firmilian and Cyprian remained unconvinced; but it is thought he retracted his opinion before his martyrdom, as his loyalty to the Popes was great. He continued to hold it during the time of St. Stephen. This great

and holy Pontiff decreed that the sacred vestments
should be worn at Mass and in the Church, but not
elsewhere, by bishops, priests, and deacons, and that
others not in holy Orders should not usurp them.
The proud and ostentatious Paul of Samosata put
forth his heresy that Christ had begun from Mary,
renewing the doctrine of Artemon that He was mere
man, and was the forerunner of Arius.

Meanwhile the persecution raged with anti-
christian violence, and twelve of the cardinal clergy
of Rome suffered martyrdom.   Their names were
Bonus, Faustus, Maurus, Primitivus, Calumniosus,
John, Cyril, Basil and Theodore, Exuperantius,
Castulus, and Honoratus ; their place of martyrdom
was near the aqueduct on the Latin road.   The
Pope was obliged to take refuge in the Catacombs.
He converted and baptised Olympius, a tribune, and
his wife Exuperia, with his son Theodulus, together
with Nemesius, a tribune whom he afterwards ordained deacon, and Symphronius and Tertullinus,
who all died martyrs.   Stephen himself gave them
solemn burial with recitation of psalms.   He miraculously restored the eyesight of Lucilla the daughter
of Nemesius, and gave her baptism.   These conver-
sions and the progress of Christianity brought upon
the Pope the fury of the persecutor, and soldiers
were sent specially to take him.   When he was
found and brought into the presence of Valerian,
according to the acts quoted by Oldoin from Baronius, the emperor said :

" Art thou the man who art trying to upset the
state of Rome, and to persuade the people com-

mitted to my charge to forsake the worship of the gods ?"

The Pope replied :

" I am not upsetting the state, but I advise all men to leave their idols and adore the true God and Jesus Christ whom He has sent."

The emperor signed his sentence of death, commanding it to be executed unless he offered sacrifice in the Temple of Mars. St. Stephen, led thither, prayed that God would destroy the temple as He destroyed the Tower of Babel. Thunder and lightning followed and the temple fell ; the soldiers fled, leaving the Pope alone, and he returned to the Catacombs, where he was found at Mass and beheaded in his chair.

Some days after the martyrdom of St. Stephen, the soldiers found the boy Tarcisius, an acolyte who was carrying the holy Eucharist. They inquired what it was he bore, and rather than betray the holy mysteries, he was beaten to death with sticks and stones, but they could discover nothing on the body.

The persecution was most violent in Alexandria, where Macrinus, the chief officer of Valerian, advised by the magicians of Egypt, conducted it. He disembowelled children to consult the entrails, and is said to have instigated Valerian to persecute the Christians. When Valerian went to the Persian war, Macrinus was sent to Rome to take his place, and aspired to the empire.

St. Stephen was martyred on the 10th of August, and his body laid in the Cemetery of Callixtus. Ho

condemned the third council of Carthage, which enjoined the renewal of baptism of heretics as well as
that of Iconium. And he added the " Gloria in Excelsis" to the Mass.   He held two ordinations, creating
three bishops, six priests, and five deacons, and was
Pope part of three years.   The See was vacant
twenty-two days.

A.D. 260.—St. Sixtus II., the first to have the
same name as a predecessor in the Holy See, an
Athenian, and a philosopher of great learning, was
chosen the twenty-fifth Pope.   The times were terrible ; for, as St. Cyprian records, Valerian had
decreed that all bishops, priests, and deacons should
be at once summarily dealt with ; that all senators,
knights, and nobles found to be Christians should be
condemned, beheaded, and their goods confiscated.

St. Cyprian, after a year's banishment to Curubis,
was brought back to Carthage and executed, in the
midst of a vast assemblage of spectators.   His con-
scientious mistake, if he still held it, has not prevented him from being honoured with St. Cornelius
in the Mass as a great saint.

During the disturbance of civil wars, the empire
had relaxed its hold in the north of Europe.   Pos-
thumus had revolted and seized upon Gaul, which
he held for ten years as master.   Victorinus succeeded him, and then Tetricus, the governor of
Aquitain, on the death of Victorinus, was proclaimed emperor by the soldiers.   The Germans,
crossing the Tyrol, entered the north of Italy, and
descended as far as Ravenna.   Valerian, occupied
in the East, imprudently accepted the invitation of

Sapor, the Persian king, to an interview, and was seized as a captive. There he received a terrible retribution for his crimes as the persecutor of the Church of God. For eight or ten years a captive slave, he served as a footstool to his captor to mount his horse; and by his successor, another Sapor, he was flayed alive, and his skin, dyed red, was kept as a trophy. Odenatus and his accomplished wife, Zenobia, Queen of Palmyra, asserted their independence, and gained from the Persians Mesopotamia, as far as Ctesiphon. Zenobia wished to be instructed in the Christian religion, but applied to the heretical Bishop of Antioch, Paul of Samosata.

The Sabellian heresy arose, which was a confused theism denying the Divinity of the Son and the Personality of the Holy Ghost. It had existed before in a different form, in the time of the great martyr Ignatius, amongst those called the Patripassians, who held that the Father suffered in the Flesh. The Sabellians were chiefly found at Ptolemais or Barce, in the Pentapolis. By these the way was being paved for the advance of the Arian and Macedonian heresies. The Millenarians, who proclaimed a reign of Christ on earth with all sensual delights, renewed the errors of Cerinthus, and were called Nepotians, from Nepos, a Bishop of Egypt, who embraced or put forth the doctrines of the sect.

St. Sixtus had been sent as Legate of the Pope to Spain, and brought back with him Lawrence, whom he created deacon of the Holy Roman Church, and Vincent, who returned to Spain. He made Genulfus, the son of Genitus, a Roman, bishop, and

6

sent him with legatine powers as a missioner to
Gaul ; and Fleury says he made Peregrinus Bishop
of Auxerre.   St. Fructuosus, Bishop of Tarragona,
suffered at this time, burned alive in the amphitheatre, with his deacons, Augurius and Eulogius ;
and St. Saturninus, at Toulouse, dragged to death
by a bull ; and some place at this time the martyrdom of St. Denis at Paris, with Rusticus and Eleutherius.   In Africa, the Martyrs of Utica, called,
from their mode of death, the " Massa Candida,"
two or three hundred in number, chose, rather than
offer incense to the idols, to fling themselves into a
burning lime-pit, where they were consumed.

The Pope, after eleven months and a few days of
Pontificate, was seized on the accusation of preaching Christianity and holding forbidden assemblies in
the Catacombs.   He was taken in the Cemetery of
Calixtus, brought before the tribunal of Macrinus,
and condemned to die.   As he was led to the place
of execution, outside of the Capenian Gate, Lawrence, the deacon, wept and made complaint :

" Where are you going, my Father, without your
son ?   You were not wont to offer the Holy Sacrifice without your deacon.   In what have I displeased
you ?   Try me, and see if I am worthy of the choice
you have made of me to dispense the Blood of the
Lord."

St. Sixtus replied, " I do not leave you nor forsake you, my son ; for you a greater combat is in
store.   I am old and feeble ; you are young, and
your triumph will be more glorious.   After three
days you will follow me."

He then commended to his care, as archdeacon, the treasures of the Church, and was beheaded, with Quartus, on the 6th of August, and was buried in the Cemetery of Calixtus. On the same day, but at a different spot, the deacons Felicissimus and Agapetus, and the sub-deacons Januarius, Magnus, Innocent, and Stephen, were martyred, and buried in the Cemetery of Prætextatus.

The Prefect of Rome demanded of Lawrence the treasures of the Church.

Lawrence replied, " It is true that the Church is rich, and that the emperor has not treasures to equal it. Give me time, and I will show you them."

The prefect gave him three days, and he gathered together the halt, the maimed, and the blind.

" Is it thus you mock me ?" said the prefect. " I know you despise death ; but you shall not die easily."

He commanded a bed of iron to be brought, and Lawrence to be laid upon it. A slow fire was kindled below. The Christians present saw the face of Lawrence grow brilliant with light, and smelt a sweet odour as his body was consumed ; but the Pagans did not perceive it. When roasted on one side, he bid them turn him on the other, and said, " It is cooked enough, and you can eat." He then raised his eyes to Heaven, and prayed to God for the conversion of Rome, and gave up his soul. There died with him four others—Severus, priest ; Claudius, sub-deacon ; Crescentius, lector ; and Romanus, door-keeper. His body was borne by senators converted by his constancy, and buried in the Ager Veranus, on the road to Tibur.

St. Sixtus created two bishops, four priests, and seven deacons. Two Epistles are attributed to him —one to Gratus, on the Eternal Generation of the Son ; and another to the Bishops of Spain, on Obedience and Unity. The See was vacant thirty-five days.

CHAPTER VIII.

A.D. 262.—There are few scenes to compare in all the world's eventful history with the endurance of Lawrence on the bars, laughing at the terrors of death. Grand and magnificent as are the pages of the Catholic Church militant, they record few examples to equal in sublimity the death of the great deacon, who is reckoned by some a cardinal archdeacon of the Holy Roman Church. What can equal, or even bear a distant similitude to, the glory of the great Mother who has given birth to such children? There is a touching pathos in the courage of boys and girls welcoming death; in the sweetness of Venantius at Camerino; of Agnes at the age of twelve, and the little Spanish boys, Justus and Pastor. But as a man is, so is his strength. David as a boy played with lions and with bears; but as a man, laughed at the Philistine. And it is this spirit—the spirit of Lawrence—which the Church sings of in her anthems when it praises him, and says that "God loves a cheerful giver." How little must the soul of that man be—or rather how blighted, like the spirit of the arch-fiend himself—

who can turn to a contemptuous sneer, or regard
with bitter sarcasm, the heroic joy in death which
has lit up with triumph in their last moments the
faces of God's martyrs! Who, with a pen dipped
in gall, can call a holy martyr who thus smiled at
death a "jester," while he affects to praise a persecuting monster, stained with pitiless bloodshed and
impurity without a name. History distilled from
such a pen is a poisonous draught, ignoring or blas-
pheming all that is grand and beautiful, and holding
up to admiration what is base and detestable.

Another dreadful martyrdom, at which the imagi-
nation recoils, is that of St. Hippolytus. Seized in
his own house, while in the act of receiving the Holy
Eucharist, by the officers of Valerian, he was first
beaten with clubs, and then, in mockery of his name,
dragged at the tails of horses through thorny places,
and rent asunder.

The twenty-sixth Pope was Dionysius, a monk or
anchorite, whose origin Pope Damasus says he could
not discover; but, according to some, he was a
native of Calabria. During his Pontificate there
was some respite from the horrors of persecution;
for Gallienus, terrified at the retribution which fell
upon Valerian, and the disasters of the empire, abstained from active measures against the Christians,
giving himself up to luxury at Rome. Plotinus, the
Neo-Platonist philosopher, was in great credit with
Gallienus, and had many admirers amongst the
Roman nobles. He pretended to have an attendant
genius, like Socrates, and derided the vulgar notions
of the heathen gods. Porphyrius, the enemy of

Christianity, was his disciple. He died of the pre-
vailing pestilence, at the age of sixty-six. St. Gregory Thaumaturgus, Bishop of Neocesarea, in Pontus,
having brought to Christianity the whole of his
people except seventeen, died also at this time.
Paul of Samosata was condemned in a council assembled at Antioch, at which Gregory, afterwards a
martyr, Bishop of Cesarea, was present. A full
account of the proceedings was sent to Pope Dionysius by Maximus of Alexandria.

Gallienus, the emperor, was summoned from Rome
in the midst of his pleasures by the news that the
army of the Upper Danube had invested Aureolus
with the imperial purple, and entered Italy. He
hastened to Milan, and besieged Aureolus ; but was
cut off by a conspiracy of his own officers. However, before he died he had time to nominate Claudius, the commander of the legions of Illyria, his
successor in the empire. Claudius, whose elder
brother, Crispus, was grandfather of Constantius
Chlorus, defeated and put to death Aureolus. He
won the title of Gothicus, by conquering in battle
an army of three hundred thousand Goths and Sarmatians. Having thinned their ranks in a series of
battles, he shut up the remainder in the passes of
the Balkan until they surrendered.

A decree of Claudius is recorded, sanctioning the
renewal of the cruelties against the Christians ; for
he gave orders that "All Christians who were
already in prison, or were found at large, should be
punished without further inquiry." In accordance
with this summary command, Marius, a noble Per-

sian, with his wife Martha, and two sons, Audifax
and Abachum, coming to Rome to venerate the
tombs of the martyrs, were apprehended and led
through the city. Their hands were cut off and
hung about their necks; they were then beheaded
at the sand-pits on the Cornelian Way, at the thirteenth mile-stone, and their bodies thrown upon a
pyre to be consumed; but their half-burned remains
were gathered by Felicitas, a Roman lady, and buried
on her estate. St. Prisca, thirteen years old, a noble
Roman girl, suffered martyrdom. Although so
young, she was thrown into prison, accused of being
a Christian, cruelly scourged, and exposed in the
amphitheatre to be devoured by a lion; but the lion
licked her feet. She was then put upon the rack,
and, after other torments, was beheaded and buried
at the tenth mile-stone on the Appian Way. The
great St. Antony about this time retired into a life
of solitude in Upper Egypt.

Pope Dionysius is given by some ten or eleven
years of Pontificate, though others give him only
six; he is thought to have died a natural death
of old age. He was buried in the Cemetery of
Calixtus, on the Appian Way, having held two
ordinations, and created seven bishops, twelve
priests, and six deacons. The See was vacant
six days.

A.D. 273.—St. Felix, a Roman, the son of Constantius, was elected twenty-seventh Pope. Claudius,
after two years of empire, died at Sirmium, and
Aurelian, a Pannonian, who had risen from the
ranks to be commander of the cavalry, was chosen

by the soldiers to succeed him. He was distinguished
for his great personal prowess, and is said, by
Theoclius, to have killed with his own hand
forty-eight Sarmatians in one day, and in other
engagements nine hundred and fifty more, so that
his legionaries in their songs celebrated him as the
slayer of a thousand. The state of the empire
demanded the aid of a warlike emperor, for it was
beset on every side. The Germans of the Upper
Danube, crossing the Alps by the Splugen Pass, had
broken into Italy, and descended as far as Fano in
Umbria. Rome was alarmed, and Aurelian, con-
sulting the Sibylline books, offered the prescribed
sacrifices. He defeated the invaders at Fano, and
again at Pavia, and drove them out of Italy.
Having saved Rome, he added to its walls, which he
made more than twenty miles in circumference. He
then turned his arms against Tetricus, the usurper
of Gaul, who reigned as emperor in Aquitain, whom
he defeated at Châlons and took prisoner. He
passed then into Asia, where he beat the armies of
Queen Zenobia, first at Antioch and then at Emesa,
and shut her up in Palmyra. Flying from thence,
she was taken captive on the banks of the Euphrates.
Aurelian triumphed, and led in his train the two
captives, Tetricus and Zenobia, but both were afterwards treated with kindness. Zenobia lived on an
estate near Tivoli, and her family was reckoned
among the nobility of Rome. Zenobius, Bishop of
Florence in the time of St. Ambrose, is thought by
Baronius to have belonged to it.

Aurelian at first seems to have favoured the

Christians, and supported the orthodox against
Paul of Samosata. Dorotheus, a learned eunuch
who was a Greek and Hebrew scholar, is said to
have been intimate with him, but being attached to
Pagan superstitions, he founded temples to the gods,
and erected a magnificent one at Rome in honour of
the sun. He issued edicts to abolish Christianity,
and the name of this great warrior is stained with
the blot of persecutor of the Church, the ninth from
Nero. He was preparing still more bloody edicts,
and was on the point of signing them when his arm
fell paralysed.

Many martyrdoms took place in Gaul, amongst
whom were St. Savinian at Troyes, St. Reverian at
Autun. At Præneste, in Italy, the boy Agapetus,
aged fifteen, refusing to deny the faith, was first cruelly
scourged, and then cast into prison and kept four
days without food. Burning charcoal was put upon
his head; he was hung with his head [downwards
over the stifling smoke of a fire, boiling water poured
upon his stomach, and his jaws broken. The judge
who gave the sentence was struck dead upon his
tribunal, but in pursuance of the imperial decrees,
the boy was flung to the wild beasts, which refused
to touch him. He was then beheaded. The
triumph of grace is most signal in tender age, and
the heroic constancy of the children in Japan,
who offered themselves in their holiday clothes to
martyrdom, makes the pages of the history
of its Christianity, otherwise so illustrious, still
more glorious. But even in Japan some pity
was accorded to the tender age of children, while

the prefects of Rome seem to have known no mercy.

Pope Felix soon fell a victim, and, according to Baronius, died a martyr after a Pontificate of two years and five months, though some give him four years. He decreed that Mass should not be said in places unconsecrated, except in case of necessity; that if the consecration of a place were doubtful, or in lapse of time forgotten, that it should receive consecration, saying that it could not be called a repetition, since it was not known to have been ever done. The decree seems to relate to the memories or sepulchres of martyrs, for the custom of the Catholic Church was ever to make use of such memorials as places for offering the Holy Sacrifice of the Mass, and in churches to place relics of martyrs under the Altars, which seems in accordance with the words in the Apocalypse : " I saw under the Altar the souls of them which were slain for the Word of God." For Catholic Ritual in many things represents the mysteries of heaven unveiled in that sublime book.

In the time of St. Felix an heresiarch arose, who was first a slave, then an adopted son of the widow of a sage in Persia, whose books and money he inherited, taking the name of Manes. He fled from Persia to Mesopotamia, to escape the king's anger at the death of the prince whom he pretended to cure. There he spread his pestilent doctrines, and left twelve disciples, teaching that the God of the Old Testament is the author of evil. He narrowly escaped being stoned to death by the people, and in his flight was caught by the soldiers of the Persian king and flayed alive. His doctrine, that there are two principles, one of good, and the other of evil, and that the Old Testament and the creation proceeded from the evil principle, long continued to spread a baneful influence over a portion of the world. Fragments of a letter from Pope Felix to Maximus, Bishop of Alexandria, against the errors of Paul of Samosata and Sabellius, are quoted by St. Cyril, and in the Council of Chalcedon. He held two ordinations, creating five bishops, nine priests, and five deacons, and was buried at the second milestone on the Aurelian Way, on the spot where he himself consecrated a church, which was afterwards dedicated to St. Pancratius, the cemetery being called after him the Cemetery of St. Felix. The See was vacant five days.

A.D. 275.—Eutychian, an Etrurian, the son of Maximus, succeeded Felix. This Pope is said to have buried with his own hands three hundred and forty-two martyrs in various cemeteries within and without the city. He decreed that martyrs should be buried in a dalmatic and a robe of purple; moreover, that fruits, and especially grapes, should be blest at the offertory, which was an ancient custom, but was renewed by him against the errors of the Manichees. According to some he was Pontiff only for one year; but others, with more probability, give him eight years, for he held five ordinations, and created nine bishops, fourteen priests, and five deacons.

The Emperor Aurelian was assassinated on the

way to the East near Byzantium. A thunderbolt
from heaven fell so close to him that the bystanders
were terrified, and shortly afterwards he was killed
by his soldiers while on the march to avenge himself
on the Persian king. For eight months the empire
was vacant, until Tacitus, an aged senator, was
chosen, who reigned for six months, and perished in
Cappadocia, succeeded by his brother Florian, slain
at Tarsus after an empire of three months. Probus,
a successful soldier and strict disciplinarian as a
military commander, was made emperor. Deterred
by the fate of Aurelian, he wished to put a stop to
the persecution, and published edicts to that effect,
but while employing his soldiers in draining the
marshes of Sirmium, he provoked a mutiny by his
severity. Flying for safety to a tower or castle
cased with iron, he was there taken and killed.
Carus, the prætorian prefect, with his sons Carinus
and Numerianus, seized upon the empire ; but Carus
died by lightning falling on his tent. Carinus,
residing at Rome, made himself odious by his vices,
though the populace was gratified with the splendour
of his entertainments in the amphitheatre. Numerian
died in Asia, and Arrius Aper, the prætorian prefect,
who kept his death for a time concealed, was suspected of his murder. The legions, putting Aper in
chains, elected Diocletian, captain of the bodyguard,
emperor. Diocletian, allowing Aper no time for
justification, stabbed him with his own hand, and
was proclaimed by the soldiers. The course of these
events occupied about the space of six years.

Pope Eutychian wrote two Epistles—one to the

Bishops of Spain, another to the Bishops of Sicily, and dedicated a church to St. Prisca on the Aventine. He was martyred in the time of Probus, and buried in the Cemetery of Calixtus, on the Appian Way. His memory is kept on the 8th of December. The See was vacant nine days.

A.D. 283.—Caius, the twenty-ninth Pope, was chosen to succeed Eutychian. He was born in Rome, but by his father's side a Dalmatian, being the son of Caius Maximus, a relative of Diocletian, and by his mother's side a Spaniard. Nor was he the only Christian of the family, for Gabinius his brother or half-brother, and Susanna his niece, were martyred, Gabinius promoted to the priesthood after the death of his wife, and Susanna choosing to die a virgin rather than submit to be espoused to Galerius Maximinus, the adopted son of Diocletian. Caius was Pope for twelve years, and during his Pontificate the great and last persecution began. He marked out anew the regions or districts of Rome, as Pope Fabian and others had done before him, assigning them to deacons to keep a register of the martyrs and record their acts, and he is said to have arranged the order of degrees by which the clergy are successively promoted in ordination—namely, door-keeper, lector, exorcist, acolyte, sub-deacon, deacon and priest—but these ranks already existed, and his decree therefore required that a bishop legitimately ordained should ascend by these degrees. He also decreed that no laic should summon a priest to trial, and that no accusation of a pagan or a heretic should be received against a Christian.

Victorinus wrote in his time commentaries on Scripture praised by St. Jerome, and Pamphilus, the relative of Eusebius of Cesarea, the admirer of Origen, wrote out a great portion of his works with a defence of them.

The empire was divided between Carinus, master of Rome, and Diocletian, supreme in the East. Carinus either held in esteem or feared the Christians, and was not inclined to persecute; but he was soon obliged to gather all his forces to encounter Diocletian. They met at Belgrade, and the armies of the East and West were hurled upon each other. Diocletian was on the point of being defeated, when Carinus was slain by an officer whom he had injured. The new emperor, assuming the name of Jovius, and changing that of Diocles to Diocletianus, chose for his colleague a ferocious Dalmatian soldier, Maximianus, who took the surname of Herculius. In these two men subtle cunning combined with brutal violence were arrayed against the Church of Christ, for though at first Diocletian dissembled his hatred, or for reasons of prudence forbore to persecute openly, Maximian soon began to display his ferocity, and by his command the Theban legion was first decimated, and then the whole massacred, when he passed into Gaul to contend with Carausius.

Pope Caius for eight years escaped death, lying in concealment, sometimes in the Catacombs and sometimes under the protection of the emperor's own chamberlain, not so much for the sake of avoiding persecution as for the support and comfort of the Christians whom he visited by night. He ordained Tranquillinus priest, and the brothers Marcus and Marcellianus deacons, and instructed and baptised Sebastian, the commander of the first cohort, whom he named Defender of the Church for his signal courage in confirming and sustaining the spirit of the martyrs. His niece Susanna refusing to be the wife of Galerius Maximin, the adopted son of Diocletian, was put to death by the tyrant, strangled in her father's house, and the Pope's brother Gabinius suffered martyrdom. In the Breviary they are commemorated with Caius on the 22nd of April, though he seems not to have died at the same time, for it is said that he dedicated the house of Gabinius, which adjoined his own, as a church, and there celebrated Mass after their martyrdom. The church had the title of St. Caius or Gabinius and Susanna. At length, being sought for and discovered, Caius was beheaded, and was buried in the Cemetery of Calixtus, at the third milestone on the Appian Way, where his body was found in the second year of Pope Gregory XV. He held four ordinations and created five bishops, twenty-five priests, and eight deacons. The See was vacant for eleven days.

CHAPTER IX.

TENTH PERSECUTION BY DIOCLETIAN.

A.D. 295.—The thirtieth Pope was Marcellinus, a Roman, the son of Projectus, who succeeded St. Caius in the Chair of Peter. Hitherto, with the exception perhaps of Dionysius alone, each one of the Pastors of the flock had been called upon to lay down his life for the sheep. This fact, if other proofs were wanting, is sufficient to show the frequency of martyrdom. For if the Holy Father, for whose life and safety all the faithful must have been solicitous and used every measure for his protection, notwithstanding had to suffer death for the faith, the expectation of such a fate must have been familiar to every true Christian. Persecution had victims almost without ceasing either at Rome or in the provinces, except in the singularly-favoured Isle of Britain, until the time of Diocletian.

But now the storm burst upon the whole world. The Beast, as it is figuratively called in the Apocalypse of St. John, and the Vision of Hermas, was roused to fury as if the time of the abridgment of its power was near. The world of heathendom

7

was not to perish without a struggle, nor the demon to lose his reign over it unavenged. The cunning of the old serpent was faithfully represented in Diocletian, and the lion's ferocity in Maximian. Gibbon paints it well when he speaks of Diocletian as "singularly mild in victory, but artful," and of Maximian as "the ready instrument of cruelty, and insensible to pity." He says ironically : "The motion of the world was maintained by the all-seeing wisdom of Jovius, and the earth purged of its monsters by the arm of Herculius." The sufferings of the Saints culminated to a climax as the time of deliverance began to draw near. Without attempting to assign the chronological order, we will follow the recorded list of the martyrs as they come in the course of the ecclesiastical year.

St. Lucy, the virgin of Syracuse, whose feast is on the 13th of December, is well named first, for besides the celebrity of her martyrdon, she prophesied the future peace of the Church on the death of Diocletian and Maximian. The next glorious name is St. Sebastian, on the 20th of January. His father was a nobleman of Narbonne, his mother a Milanese, and he was dear to Diocletian as a soldier, being appointed by him commander of the first cohort. He was a Christian in secret, until he was discovered by his kindness to the martyrs and his exhortations to them to be firm. This was especially noticed in the dreadful martyrdom of Marcus and Marcellianus, and reported to the emperor. St. Sebastian's lingering and double martyrdom is sufficiently well known. St. Agnes, on the following day, is equally famous, and it is needless to repeat her familiar story. The forty martyrs in Armenia, whose feast is on the 10th of March, suffered later under Licinius, towards the close of the great persecution. They were placed naked on a frozen lake to perish of cold, with a warm bath ready for such as would recant. One who yielded was replaced by the sentinel on guard, who saw an angel descend from heaven, bearing forty celestial crowns. Pancratius, a Phrygian boy of fourteen, who came to Rome, was baptised by the Pope, and refusing to renounce the faith, was beheaded and buried on the Aurelian Way. His festival is on the 12th of May. Peter the exorcist, who freed his gaoler's daughter from the devil, with Marcellinus, the priest who baptised her and her family, together with the Bishop Erasmus, clothed by Maximian in a red-hot coat of mail, suffered on the 2nd of June. The two brothers, Primus and Felician, are commemorated on the 9th. Felician, tied by his hands and feet to a stake, was left hanging for three days without food. His brother Primus was told by the prætor that Felician had recanted, and was honoured by the emperors. " I have learned," said Primus, " from an angel what has been done to my brother, and I would I were in the same martyrdom with him whom I love so dearly." The prætor, bringing in Felician, poured into the mouth of Primus molten lead. Both were then cast to the lions, who fawned upon them, and five hundred converts were made by the miracle, who embraced Christianity with their families. Primus and Felician were beheaded. On the 15th of June four Roman soldiers, Basilides,

Cyrinus, Nabor, and Nazarius, confessing to be Christians, were thrown into a dark dungeon. As they prayed, light filled the prison, and Marcellus, the keeper of the prison, was converted, with many others. They were scourged with lashes armed with hooks, and after seven days brought before the emperor and beheaded.

Cyriacus, the deacon, who delivered Artemia, the daughter of Diocletian, from possession, with Sisinnius, Largus, and Smaragdus, suffered on the 8th of August. Cyriacus was dragged in chains before Maximian's chariot, and then racked. Boiling pitch was then poured upon him. They were finally beheaded, with twenty others, near the gardens of Sallust, on the Salarian Way, and their bodies were first entombed there, but afterwards, in the time of Pope Marcellus, the lady Lucina, wrapping their bodies in linen with precious unguents, buried them at the seventh milestone on the Ostian Way.

On the 12th of August, Tiburtius, the son of Chromatius, prefect of the city, converted by St. Sebastian, declaring himself a Christian, was ordered by Fabian, the judge, either to sacrifice to the gods or walk barefoot upon burning coals. Tiburtius, making the sign of the Cross, walked upon the coals, saying; "See by this that the God whom the Christians worship is the true God, for the glowing coals seem to me a bed of flowers." The judge, attributing it to magic art, commanded him to be led out of the city and beheaded. He was buried at the third milestone on the Lavicanian Way. Susanna, the virgin daughter of Gabinius, the Pope's brother, suffered on the same day, cruelly murdered in her father's house for refusing the nuptials of Galerius Maximinus, commemorated with Pope Caius on the 22nd of April.

On the 31st, St. Felix, who spit upon the idols, suffered with Adauctus, so called because he raised his voice from the crowd to declare himself a Christian as Felix was led to execution. Adauctus is almost the only victim of the long list whom the scoffing Gibbon singles out to name.

In September there follow Gorgonius, at Nicomedia, chamberlain of Diocletian; Euphemia, at Chalcedon, exposed to wild beasts; and Lucia, a widow, of Rome, accused of being a Christian by her son. She was put in a caldron of pitch and molten lead, from which she came forth unhurt, and, converting the noble Geminianus, was beheaded. On the 19th, St. Januarius, whose blood is still miraculous, suffered with his companions at Naples; and at Agaunum, in Valais, St. Maurice, with the Theban legion, which was first decimated for refusing to sacrifice, and finally, by order of Maximian, the whole of the remainder surrounded by the imperial troops and destroyed.

SS. Cosmas and Damian are remembered with special honour in the Mass. They were noble Arabian brothers, physicians to Diocletian and Maximin in their diseases. They had the gift of healing most incurable disorders. Being put to the most refined tortures, they remained firm. Thrown into the sea, tied hand and foot, they came out with their bonds loosed. Accused of magic art, they were thrown into the fire, and when the fire refused to consume them, they were beheaded. Their feast is on the 27th of September.

Vitalis, a slave, and Agricola, his master, a gentleman of Bologna, are commemorated the same month. Vitalis, tortured for a long time to induce his master to yield, was crucified with red-hot nails; Agricola was confirmed by his slave's constancy and example. They were buried in the Jews' Catacomb at Milan, and translated from thence by St. Ambrose.

The four Coronati, or martyr-crowned brothers— so called because their names were long unknown— Severus, Severianus, Carpophorus, and Victorinus, are commemorated on the 8th of November. They were beaten to death and their bodies flung to dogs, which refused to touch them, and entombed at the third milestone on the Lavicanian Way, near the sepulchre of five other martyrs in the same persecution, Claudius, Nicostratus, Symphorianus, Castorius, and Simplicius, sculptors, who refused to make statues of the heathen gods. These were shut up alive in leaden coffins and thrown into the Tiber. The relics both of the four and five were afterwards placed in the Church of the Quatuor Coronati, built in the city.

Theodore, a soldier, suffered on the 10th of November for setting fire to a temple, condemned to be burned alive; and on the 11th is the memory of Mennas, an Egyptian, who, from a soldier becoming a hermit, leapt into the amphitheatre in Phrygia, where the games were held in honour of the emperor's birthday, protesting against the foul and impious superstitions of Cybele, and was put to death with great torments. The body of Mennas was afterwards taken to Constantinople.

Chrysogonus, after two years imprisonment at Rome, was sent for by Diocletian to Aquileia, and there interrogated " If he would consent to worship the gods ?" at the same time the emperor offered him honours.

Chrysogonus replied, " I worship the true God in my heart, and I praise Him with my mouth. The gods that are the images of devils I detest and abominate." He was beheaded on the 24th of November.

We may close the list of these more celebrated martyrdoms with St. Catherine of Alexandria, the victim of Maximin the nephew of Galerius, and St. Peter, the great bishop who foretold the apostasy of Arius. But besides these, multitudes of known martyrs might be added, for the persecution raged over the whole Roman world. Britain was not excepted, and was for the first time disturbed in its peaceful Christianity. St. Alban, an official at Verulam, converted by Amphibalus, died to protect his instructor. SS. Julius and Aaron are the only names recorded at Caerleon, but it is said that to escape the violence of the persecution, the Christians concealed themselves in dens and caves, and the number massacred at Lichfield gave it the name of the Field of Corpses. At Saragossa, in Spain, the Bishop Valerius was martyred with a vast number of companions, and the deacon St. Vincent, like his companion St. Lawrence, was laid upon a gridiron and roasted alive. At Complutum two little boys at school, Justus and Pastor, defied the scourge and other torments and were beheaded. In Asia the great martyr St. George, whose acts when freed from falsifications of heretics are now defended, endured unheard-of torments, and at the command of the tyrant walked in red-hot shoes.

In the plains of Palestine multitudes were exposed naked to wild beasts, and a whole city in Phrygia was consumed in flames with its inhabitants because they refused to sacrifice to the false gods. Pope Damasus relates that within thirty days seventeen thousand martyrs suffered, besides those who were condemned to the mines or to labour in the quarries, some with one foot dislocated or hamstrung behind the knee, and some with the sinews of the left leg cauterised or seared with red-hot irons. Theodoret tells us that an edict was proclaimed commanding the destruction of every Christian church throughout the world, to be executed on a Good Friday. Such was the persecution in which infidel writers can find but few names to record. Diocletian boasted in an inscription that he had stamped out Christianity from the world. He was superstitious and timid, and in some sacrificial rites received responses from the demons which led him to dread Christians. He chose for his assistant in the East a Pannonian herdsman, Galerius, a man whose very sight inspired terror, whom he invested with the purple and the title of Cæsar. Perhaps he chose him as a match for Maximian in ferocity, but he soon learned to be afraid of him, though at first he had ventured to treat him with contumely, making him follow behind his chariot on foot for having suffered a defeat in Persia. Galerius Maximinus was the type of a true persecutor, pitiless and horribly licentious. Under such emperors faith and chastity had no resource but to die. Christians holding offices were disgraced, soldiers cashiered and then martyred ; one who tore down an edict was skinned alive. Eyes were torn out and replaced with coals, sharp reeds were run into the most sensitive parts, and every imaginable torment was employed.

No wonder that fear invaded the very sanctuary. Pope Marcellinus was led to the sacrifice in the temple of Isis, and there, through fear or compulsion, offered two grains of incense. Three priests and two deacons accompanied the Pope to the door, and some Christians were present in the temple at the action, which they witnessed and reported. So it said in the acts, and though St. Augustin does not admit it, arguing against Petilian, it seems probable that in a moment of weakness, like St. Peter, Marcellinus fell ; and afterwards, when an assembly of bishops was held at Sinuessa, he presented himself as a penitent clothed in sackcloth, with ashes on his head. No one dared to condemn him, saying, " Judge and pronounce on thy own cause. The chief See is judged by none." " Peter also fell, and wept for his sin." Marcellinus would have abdicated, but his abdication was not received. He returned to Rome, and presented himself before the emperor to die. Before he suffered, he begged of the Priest Marcellus not to lay his body in the tomb, as un-

worthy of burial.   He was martyred together with
Claudius, Cyrinus and Antoninus, and their bodies
lay for thirty-six days in the public way unburied.
St. Peter appeared to Marcellus in a dream, and
commanded the body of the martyred Pope to be
entombed.   It was buried in the Cemetery of
Priscilla.   Marcellinus held the Pontificate nine
years and two months, and in two ordinations created
five bishops, four priests, and two deacons.   The See
was vacant twenty-five days.

A.D. 303.—Marcellus, a Roman, the son of Benedictus of the Region via Lata, succeeded Marcellinus,
with whom by some he has been erroneously confounded.   At Rome, during the space of seven years,
the Baths of Diocletian were building on the
Quirinal, chiefly by the hands of Christian confessors condemned to slavery.   The immense pile
still in part remains to attest the magnificence of
Rome in the days of imperial luxury, and to give a
portion of its halls to form the Church of Our Lady
of the Angels.   Diocletian, at the same time with
Galerius, investing with the imperial purple Constantius Chlorus, gave him the title of Cæsar ; and
Maximian, bestowing on him his daughter-in-law
Theodora for wife, adopted him as his son.   Constantius, divorcing Helena, the mother of Constantine,
had a young family by Theodora, and ruled in Gaul
and Britain.   Thus the empire was divided into
four parts, Maximian residing for the most part at
Milan, and Diocletian at Nicomedia.

In the year 305, Diocletian, having assumed the
Eastern tiara and triumphed at Rome, retired to

Nicomedia, sick and ill at ease. He was in mortal dread of Galerius, and at his suggestion or command resigned the empire, returning to his native place, Dalmatia, where he built a palace of great size and magnificence. On the same day, by agreement, Maximian resigned the empire at Milan, and retired to a villa in Lucania. The terrible Galerius, as Lactantius relates in the eighteenth chapter on the death of persecutors, was the cause of this extraordinary step, and the panegyric of Gibbon is wasted on the humility of Diocletian. Galerius was the Master of the East, and would doubtless remember that once he had run behind the chariot of the tyrant. Severus was created by him Cæsar and ruler of Italy ; but Maxentius, the son of Maximian, having gained the Prætorian guard, was master of Rome. Although Maxentius was the husband of his daughter, Galerius was much enraged at this, but he could not prevent it.

The number of Christians in Rome was now very considerable, and Pope Marcellus divided the city into twenty-five parishes or titles. The explanation of the origin of these has been already given, and the cardinalate shown to be contemporary with the Papacy. The division by Marcellus means that he carried out the work of previous Popes, especially of Cletus, Evaristus and Hyginus, for by command of St. Peter, Cletus is said to have ordained twenty-five priests. The district parishes defined by Marcellus, to which five were added, the title of Equitius by St. Silvester, and four more by succeeding Pontiffs, remained without change, being in all twenty-eight ancient titles, down to the time of Sixtus the Fourth.

The widow Lucina having given her property for the use of the Church, Maxentius was informed of it. He summoned the Pope Marcellus to his presence, and commanded him to give up the Pontificate and the name of Christian. Upon his refusal he was beaten with clubs, and then, for his degradation, made the keeper of a public stable or stall of beasts. In this condition the Pope, neither omitting his prayers or fasts nor his attention to the government of the parishes of the city, directed everything by letters. After nine months' captivity he was delivered by night, and concealed in the house of Lucina, whose dwelling had been dedicated as a church. There Marcellus was found officiating, and by order of Maxentius the beasts in public employment were brought into it, and the Pope again put to menial service to litter and attend to them, until he died of the confinement, fetor and filth. The Church of St. Marcellus is built on the site of the house of Lucina, where the Pope kept the stall of beasts. His body was buried in the Cemetery of Priscilla, on the Salarian Way. He was Pope for five years and six months, and ordained twenty-one bishops, twenty-six priests, and two deacons.

Galerius and his nephew Maximin continued the persecution in the East, and St. Dorothea was put to death by Theophilus, the prefect of Cesarea in Cappadocia. The prefect taunted her, and asked her to send him some of the fruits of the paradise to which she was going. The virgin martyr promised to do so, and the prefect was visited by an angel bringing roses and apples of exquisite taste and perfume at the season of the year when they could not naturally be obtained ; he was converted to Christianity and died a martyr.

The martyrdoms in Egypt continued for years with great cruelties, especially in the Thebaid, and some were torn asunder by bending down the trees, which were suddenly loosed with the limbs tied to them. But it is time to close the curtain upon these scenes of suffering, for the three centuries allotted to the Church of the Catacombs are drawing to an end, and the day begins to dawn after the long night of persecution.

CHAPTER X.

A.D. 309.—Eusebius, a Greek, the son of a physician, was chosen Pope to succeed Marcellus, who, according to St. Damasus, was exiled from Rome during part of his Pontificate; and this is confirmed from some ancient records by Bollandus. In the life of Eusebius, Bishop of Vercellæ, it is said that he was brought to Rome by his mother, Restituta, a Sardinian lady, and baptised by Pope Eusebius, who gave the child his own name. Eusebius of Cesarea, of dubious Catholicity, who is said to have denied the faith in the persecution, wrote his " Ecclesiastical History" about this time, and the life of the martyr Pamphilus; and Lactantius, the disciple of Arnobius, taught a school of rhetoric at Nicomedia, but having few scholars, composed many works against the Pagans and in praise of Christianity. In his old age he was tutor to Crispus, the son of Constantine.

Maxentius, proclaimed emperor by the Prætorian Guard, invited Maximian to come to Rome from his retreat in Lucania. Upon this he wrote to Diocletian to follow his example and recover the empire; but the old wily statesman was too feeble or too sagacious to be lured from his last hiding-hole at Salona. Maximian, restored to public life, attempted to corrupt the soldiery in his own favour, and was nearly caught and killed by them with the connivance of his own son. He fled to Illyria, and from thence in fear of Galerius to Constantine.

Constantius Chlorus died at York—a man without reproach in an age of iniquity. An anecdote is recorded of him betokening a prince gifted with spirit and discernment. He retained in his service the Christians who had been true to their religion upon a trial to which he purposely put them, and dismissed those who had been false, saying "that men who were true to their God would be true to their master." Constantine was about eighteen years of age when Chlorus, his father, was made Cæsar, and was serving as tribune under Galerius in the East. The tyrant was jealous of him, and when he was sent for by his father, endeavoured to detain him. According to an author quoted by Photius, he was exposed, under honourable pretext, to a combat with a Sarmatian gladiator and a lion. Galerius, having given permission to him to travel, intended to cancel it the next day : but in the night Constantine, having received his permit, left Nicomedia, and taking the public relays of horses, travelled with wonderful celerity through Bithynia and Thrace, and across Europe to Boulogne. In person he was tall and handsome, expert and dexterous in all exercises, and prudent and chaste as well as brave. On the death of his father he was hailed Emperor of the West by the legions, to which title he succeeded by right, as his father for the last two years was styled Imperator ; but he preferred the humbler name of Cæsar, and at the age of thirty-two entered Gaul with his army, to protect the bank of the Rhine. He sent messengers to inform Maxentius of his succession, and wished to be at peace with him, for Maximian met him at Arles and gave him his daughter Fausta in marriage ; and to cope with Galerius and the power of the East, it seemed necessary that the West should be united.

Maxentius treated his proposals with indignity and bid him defiance. He had been successful in corrupting the soldiers of the Cæsar Severus sent against him by Galerius, and Severus died at Ravenna. Then Galerius himself, at the head of the Eastern legions, prepared to invade Italy and besiege Rome ; but his soldiers demurred, and he retreated. He survived his disappointed revenge some three years, but the hand of God was heavy upon him. His monstrous unwieldy body was incurably diseased, breeding lice and worms, and its stench insupportable. Before he died he issued an edict with a sullen retraction of the persecution of the Christians. He left the East divided between Licinius in Illyria, and Maximin Daia, his brutal nephew, in Asia.

Diocletian was invited to be present at Arles at the nuptials of Constantine and Fausta, but he refused to come, and then, timid and despairing, ended his life, as it is supposed, by poison. Even his admirer, Gibbon, allows that when he resigned the empire at Nicomedia to retire to Salona, and made his last appearance in public, his countenance was so ghastly and pale that he could hardly be recognised.

Maximian could not refrain from schemes of aggrandisement. In the absence of Constantine—summoned to war with the Franks—Maximian spread a report of his death, seized upon his treasures, which he distributed to the soldiers, and took the title of emperor; but surprised by Constantine before he could consolidate his power, he fled to Marseilles, and there was either most deservedly put to death, or, as is said, strangled himself with his own hands. Such was the end of the three persecutors—an example to mankind, that even in this world chastisement awaits the open enemies of Christ and His Church.

Meanwhile Maxentius filled Rome with violence and rapacity. He was avaricious, cruel, and so licentious, that a Christian lady, Sophronia, stabbed herself to preserve her chastity. The Prætorian Guard, raised to its old evil eminence and establishment, was the support of his tyranny. At one time he is said to have pretended to favour the Christians, and Pope Eusebius is thought to have died a natural death. The number of Christians in Rome was so great, that policy most probably prevented him from open persecution. But he was superstitious in the extreme, and, in his fear of Constantine, inquired into futurity by diabolical rites of divination, cutting open infants, and even it is said out of their mother's womb.

Pope Eusebius held but one ordination in the

8

month of December, creating fourteen bishops,
thirteen priests, and three deacons. He was Pope,
according to the best authorities, only one year and
seven months, and was buried in the Cemetery of
Callixtus on the Appian Way. The See was vacant
but one day, or, as Oldoin says, for seven.

A.D. 311.—Melchiades or Miltiades, an African,
or, as some say, a Spaniard by birth, a cardinal
presbyter of the Holy Roman Church, was elected
Pope—the thirty-third in the chair of Peter. He
passed decrees against the Manichees, and forbade
fasting on Sundays and Thursdays, in opposition to
heathen observances on those days. Assisted by
St. Silvester, he buried Timotheus, a cardinal priest
who suffered martyrdom, and he himself is styled a
martyr.

Constantine, invited by the senate and people of
Rome, who were weary of Maxentius, crossed the
Alps by Mont Cenis, and descended into Italy. It
is said that before he resolved upon this step—while
he deliberated at Treves on the war and his chances
of success—he saw at midday the apparition of a
luminous cross above the sun with the legend, " By
this conquer," and that he was instructed in a vision
by night in the meaning of it, to fight under the
banner of Christ. It is certain that the standard,
or " Labarum," was a pike with a transverse beam,
from which depended a veil of silk, and on the summit
was a coronet of gold, enclosing the sacred mono-
gram, which combined the figure of the cross with
the Holy Name, for medals exist of it with the
inscription, " By this conquer," and it became the

standard of the imperial legions. Eusebius, although he passes over the miracle in his history, relates it in his "Life of Constantine," and says of the banner that it spread terror and dismay in the ranks of the enemies. He declares that he heard the account of the vision from the emperor's own mouth, attesting the truth of it in the most solemn manner, though he adds, to his own shame, for he was a lukewarm Catholic, if a Catholic at all, that he would not have otherwise believed it. The banner, he says, was entrusted to fifty chosen men, and inspired invincible courage in the soldiers. There was something extraordinary in the successes of Constantine. He was met at Turin by a superior force of horsemen in complete armour, but he defeated them and cut them to pieces. Again at Verona, Pompeianus, the general of Maxentius, met him with a similar body of troops, far superior to his own in numbers. Constantine, performing exploits of great personal valour, discomfited it, and took an immense number of captives. He then marched to the Saxa Rubra, nine miles from Rome, and found Maxentius prepared to give him battle with an army still more numerous than those he had defeated at Turin and Verona, amounting, according to Zosimus, to a hundred and seventy thousand.

Forced to come out into the field, Maxentius had consulted the Sibylline books and received an answer: "That on that day the enemy of the Romans would perish." The cavalry in complete mail formed the strength of his army. Constantine charged these in person and routed them. The Prætorian Guard fought with desperation, and died on the ground it covered. The rest of the troops fled, and were driven by thousands into the Tiber. Maxentius, endeavouring to escape into the city by the Milvian Bridge, was forced by the crowd into the river, and drowned by the weight of his armour.

Constantine entered Rome A.D. 312, and remained for two or three months. He abolished for ever the Prætorian Guard, and destroyed their fortified camp, thus putting an end to the political power of that proud licentious soldiery, and delivering Rome from an incubus, but at the same time diminishing its importance as a seat of empire. He was soon called to contend with Licinius, who divided with him the world. But first they met at Milan and published an edict forbidding the persecution of the Christian religion, and this became the law of the empire.

Maximin Daia continued to the last the persecution in the East, distinguished above all other persecutors for brutal licentiousness. He died a horrible death. Having vowed to Jupiter to exterminate the Christian name if he gained the victory, he engaged in battle with Licinius. Being utterly defeated, he fled by the passes of Mount Taurus to Tarsus. There in desperation he first feasted to the full, and then swallowed poison, which, owing to his repletion, took very slow effect, and for four days he rolled on the ground in agony, beating his head against the walls. In his tortures he cried out to Christ for mercy, exclaiming that his bowels were burning as with fire, and so, howling aloud like a beast of prey, he expired.

Pope Melchiades held a council against the schismatic Donatus, at which nineteen bishops were present, and amongst them Cæcilian, the Bishop of Carthage. The Donatists appealed to Constantine, who referred them to the Pope and the Council. It is said that it was held in the Lateran, in the house of Fausta, which Constantine had given to the Pope as a residence. The schismatics were condemned, and revenged themselves by fabricating false charges against Melchiades.

The Edict of Milan not only gave liberty of worship to the Christians, but enacted that all places and properties which had been seized or confiscated belonging to Christian communities should be restored to them without dispute and without delay, and enjoined officials to see that this was executed. It is important to note this, for donations made to the Church, especially in Rome, were already very considerable.

Melchiades held only one ordination in December, creating twelve bishops of various Sees, and in the city of Rome fourteen priests and five deacons. He was Pontiff for two years, according to Baronius, though others give him three, and he was buried in the Cemetery of Callixtus, being styled a martyr, and commemorated on the 10th of December. He probably suffered martyrdom in an outbreak of Pagan animosity, for it is said that when the augurs were restored to their official duty by an imperial edict, they raised a tumult against the Christians under pretext of a lustration of the city, and that on this account St. Silvester retired for safety to Mount

Soracte. The See was vacant for seventeen days.

A.D. 314.—St. Silvester, the son of Rufinus, a Roman, was educated for the priesthood by his holy mother, Justa, and made cardinal priest by Pope Marcellinus. He was elected, on account of his consummate virtues, twenty-fourth Pope, and held the Pontificate for twenty-two years, during which a change came over the face of the world, inaugurated by laws bespeaking the influence of Christianity.

The emperors of the West had resided at Milan, and Constantine issued his first edict from thence; but about the fifth or sixth year of Pope Silvester he visited Rome, and issued new laws of the greatest importance, sitting in the Ulpian Basilica in the Forum of Trajan. It was the custom of the emperors by ancient precedent from the time of Augustus to renew every ten years their authority by the voice of the senate and people, and this custom was observed by Constantine. These, his laws, betoken a religious and Christian spirit. First he decreed the free and public exercise of divine worship by throwing open the churches and closing the temples, and that Sunday should be observed and public business cease on the first day of the week; that Christians should have power to manumit their slaves without legal process; and that marriage should be held sacred, and concubinage strictly forbidden. He forbade the exposing of infants to die, and made provision for poor parents to maintain their children, in order to prevent this horrible custom; and to protect female virtue, he enacted that those guilty of offering violence to it, and even of seduction under false pretences, should be given to the wild beasts or burned alive.

The infidel may sneer at the tone of severity of these laws protecting chastity, but they proclaim that the reign of justice and humanity, and, above all, chastity, had begun. It is the voice of Christianity, and the sound of a sweet note above the world's uproar, inaugurating the reign of the Son of the Virgin. The old world knew nothing of virginity or the sacred smile of infancy. The freedom of the slave is another sublime note betokening a change in the destinies of mankind, giving the death-blow to the horrors of the amphitheatre and proclaiming the opening of the ergastula, or the slave-prisons of Rome. The keeping of the Lord's Day, the elevation of the married state, and consequently of domestic life and the family, the protection of maidenly honour, the saving of the infant in its helplessness, the liberation of the slave, the closing of the amphitheatre, is like the proclamation of the Great Jubilee to the world, weary as it was of bloodshed, tyranny, and superstition.

It is strange, and something marvellous to believe, as some would have us, that Constantine was no Christian. It is out of the scope of this work to enter into discussions which alone would involve voluminous research and labour. The objections against the Catholic tradition are founded chiefly on some passages of Zosimus, a heathen, and Eusebius, an Arian, who is of doubtful faith in Catholic matters.

Constantius Chlorus was chaste, and of such virtue
and wisdom that he may be suspected of at least
Christian leanings. Helena, the mother of Constantine, was his wife, for Maximian stipulated for a
divorce. The story that she was an unchaste
daughter of an innkeeper of Drepanum, coming
from the pen of a heathen, is a fiction untenable in
chronology, as proved by Baronius and Alford. The
more generally received tradition is that she was of
royal British extraction. Constantine, like his father,
was chaste, and was married early to Minervina,
from whom he had a son, Crispus. She was dead
when he married Fausta, for no divorce was required,
and no one has accused him of incontinence. The tradition supported by Anastasius, two councils, and two
Popes, Gregory of Tours and others, is, that he was
baptised by St. Silvester, and for his want of faith and
temporising in embracing it, after the benefits he had
received, he was struck with leprosy, of which he was
cured in baptism. The account that he deferred it
until he should receive it in the river Jordan is, as
Platina observes, an improbable story.

After his final victory over Licinius in the great
battle of Hadrianople, in which with inferior numbers he defeated an army of a hundred and fifty
thousand men, A.D. 324, Constantine, sole emperor
of the Roman world, by letters circular, invited all
his subjects to imitate his example and embrace the
Christian faith. He could hardly have done this
unless he were himself a Christian, nor if he were
only a catechumen could he have spoken of himself as he did in a public discourse, according to

Eusebius, as a partaker in the Christian mysteries.

The following year the council was assembled at Nice for the condemnation of Arius, presided over by Hosius and the Roman priests, Victor and Vincent ; and this was done at the expense of the emperor, who provided the bishops with means of travelling, and received them at a banquet after the council. In all this we see the Christian emperor, and he shewed moreover his filial submission to the Church in refusing to listen to the complaints of bishops who preferred them to him, saying that " His was not the tribunal of appeal in things pertaining to God." He is called by St. Ambrose a holy emperor, and the Greeks account him a saint.

Even the enemies of Constantine acknowledge his extraordinary bravery. With only twelve horsemen he swam the Hebrus before his army to encourage them to meet Licinius. He was blamed by his own officers in the battle of Verona for endangering his life, and, like the soldiers of David, they entreated him not to expose himself to such a risk again. The blot of his life is the death of Crispus in the twentieth year of his reign ; but if, as Gibbon allows, it was brought about by the cruel false accusation of his stepmother, Fausta, it is an instance of Constantine's extreme severity in crimes against chastity. When he discovered, too late, the innocence of his son and the falsehood of Fausta, he justly condemned her to death. By Fausta he had three sons, Constantinus, Constantius, and Constans. The half brother of Constantine, Julius Constantius, had two sons, Gallus, and Julian afterwards the emperor and the apostate.

St. Silvester confirmed the decrees of the Council of Nice in an assembly of bishops at Rome, and about the same time, a year after the Council of Nice, according to many authors, St. Helena discovered the Holy Cross at Jerusalem, part of which she brought to Rome and placed in the Basilica, which from thence derives its title. Constantine is said to have been at that time in Rome, and as she was of great age, being eighty years old, dying soon after, she was buried in a mausoleum on the Lavicanian Way, at the Church of the Martyrs, Marcellinus and Peter, built and endowed by her son.

Nicephorus relates that after the session of Constantine in the Ulpian Basilica, twelve thousand Romans received baptism from St. Silvester, without reckoning women and children, and the Pope, holding a council, decreed that the holy chrism should be consecrated by a bishop, and that confirmation should be given to those who had received heretical baptism on their reconciliation : that priests should anoint with chrism at baptism, and the deacons at Mass wear the dalmatic with a stole on the left shoulder ; that the priest's alb, or vestment, should be of white linen, without admixture of coloured work ; that priests should not have women residing in their household, except they were their mothers, sisters, or aunts ; and the clergy should not be summoned before a lay tribunal.

It is said that a crown or jewelled diadem was

offered to the Pope by Constantine, but that he preferred to wear a Phrygian mitre woven of silk and gold, which was preserved in the Church of St. Martin in Montibus. Also it is said that the emperor offered him the government of Italy.

Councils were held in the Pontificate of St. Silvester at Arles, at Ancyra, Neocæsarea, and Alexandria and Rome, besides others which did not receive the Pope's approbation. The Œcumenical Council of Nice was presided over by Hosius, Bishop of Corduba, legate apostolic, and two cardinal priests of Rome, Victor and Vincent. Arius was condemned, and out of three hundred and eighteen bishops, six who followed his heresy were deprived of their sees. St. Athanasius was present at the council.

The decrees of the Popes on keeping Easter upon the Sunday following the fourteenth day of the moon in March were promulgated to the world, and it was acknowledged that the Pope's approbation was required to give force to the decrees of a council.

St. Silvester held six ordinations in the month of December, creating sixty-five bishops of various sees, and forty-two priests of the city of Rome, and twenty-six deacons. He was Pope, according to some, for twenty-three, but according to Baronius, twenty-one years and ten months. He was buried in the Cemetery of Priscilla on the Salarian Way, but his body was afterwards translated by Sergius II. to the Church of St. Silvester in Montibus,

built by him under the title of Equitius, and endowed by Constantine. After his death, which is
commemorated on the 31st of December, in the
year of Our Lord 335, the See was vacant for
fifteen days.

CHAPTER XI.

THE Roman Church was already rich by private donations, and was able to assist other churches. As instances of what must have been much more frequent, St. Pudentiana and St. Praxedes gave their house in the Via Patricia for a church, and St. Cecilia her house in the Trastevere. The martyrdom of Pope Marcellus was caused by his refusal to give up to Maxentius the property which the widow Lucina had given to the Church. The titular churches were those which had funds to support them, and when the Edict of Constantine came into force these possessions became legal, and the restitutions made must have been considerable. Moreover, it was appointed that certain tributes should be paid over in perpetuum to the clergy, and in order that priests and widows might receive endowments, the law was taken away forbidding unmarried persons to inherit property after the age of twenty-five.

That Constantine gave the Pope the rule over Italy is treated as a figment by Protestant writers, and looked upon with doubt and suspicion by others;

but the learned Gretser defends it, with Baronius and Cardinal Torquemada. It does not follow because the instrument of the so-called donation is fictitious or inaccurate, that therefore nothing was given.

The munificence of Constantine as a founder of churches was great, as attested by Eunapius, a Greek and a heathen, who says " that most august temples were overthrown throughout the world, and Christian churches built by him in their stead, and the expenses paid out of the imperial treasury." Sigonius, in the " History of Italy," a writer of very high authority, says that he gave to the Church " not only vessels and gifts in gold, but rich posses- sions in landed property" (Hist. Regn. Ital.).

Some of these endowments must be instanced as given by Platina and Ciaconi.

To the church in the gardens of Equitius—founded as a titular church by St. Silvester—he gave a golden chalice and other vessels of silver and gold, and an estate in Sabinum for its support, and a house and gardens within the city.

He gave the Lateran Palace, and built the Church of St. Saviour, which, with its ornaments and statues of massive silver, was most costly. The estate of Bassus, in the ager Coranus, was given for its support, with houses and gardens in the city and lands in Greece and Africa.

He built the Vatican Basilica in honour of St. Peter. The relics of the Apostle were enclosed in a vast mass of brass mixed with copper, and placed beneath the tomb, over which was erected a cross of gold weighing a hundred and fifty pounds. Besides other holy vessels, he gave three chalices of gold, and for endowment, possessions in Antioch, and revenues from gardens, mills, baths, and shops in Rome.

He built the Basilica of St. Paul on the Ostian Way, where the body of that Apostle was placed, enclosed in brass in a similar manner to that of St. Peter. He gave the same weight of vessels in gold and silver, and a cross of gold over the tomb weighing a hundred and fifty pounds. Revenues were given to it from Tarsus, in Cilicia, and from Tyre. This Basilica was enlarged by the Emperor Honorius, the son of Theodosius.

The Basilica, afterwards entitled St. Cross, in Jerusalem, was built by him and endowed with the lands of the Sessorian Palace, to receive the portion of the Holy Cross brought by his mother, St. Helena, which he enclosed in a case of silver adorned with jewels and gold. Also the Church of St. Lawrence out of the walls was built and endowed by him with lands in Agro Verano.

At the request of his daughter, Constantia, the Church of St. Agnes was built by him, with a baptistry where his sister and his daughter, Constantia, were baptised, and was endowed with lands at Fidenæ. The Church of Marcellinus and Peter the exorcist, Martyrs, where his mother, St. Helena, was buried, was endowed with Messana and the Isle of Sardinia.

To these must be added the church at Ostia, which he endowed with lands at Ardea, and the churches at Capua and Naples.

This will suffice to make good the words of
Sigonius, that Constantine gave rich possessions of
land, and he adds that in almost all the provinces of
Europe and Africa there were possessions of the
Patrimony of St. Peter ; so that without entering
into discussion as to the mode in which it was
granted, the Pope had in possession from the third
or fourth century, lands which were afterwards called
" the Patrimony," in Lombardy, Tuscany, Sabinum,
Calabria, and Sicily, and rectors or administrators of
these estates were sent by the Pope, as we find in
the letters of St. Gregory the Great. This continued until the Lombard kings invaded these possessions and despoiled the Pope ; but they were
compelled to disgorge their prey by Pepin and the
Franks, who "*restored*" to the Pope the Pentapolis, Ravenna, and Emilia, which implies previous
possession.

Soon after the great battle of Hadrianople and
the taking of Byzantium, Constantine fixed upon
that city as his imperial residence. The walls and
principal edifices were built in a few years, and,
according to some, in a few months, and the second
or new Rome was dedicated in the year 330. Here
again Constantine built the magnificent Church of
the Twelve Apostles, whilst he built others at Antioch,
Jerusalem, and Hebron ; and in the Holy Land, according to Nicephorus, he built thirty-two churches,
so that indeed he may be styled a munificent founder
of the Church in all the world.

Sozomenus says that " He gave certain tributes
accustomed to be paid to the imperial treasury by

cities and provinces to the Church and clergy in perpetuum," so that thus everywhere the Catholic
Church began to be supreme. For the Church only
requires to be free to be strong, and, without process
of installation, the removal of the seat of empire from
Rome made the Pope and Christianity dominant in
Italy. Naturally, and without effort, when the
temporal power was moved away, as if to make room,
the kingdom of God took its position above the
fragments of the old heathen fabric, and the Pope
became the prominent figure in the world ruling in
the Eternal City. The reign of the saints, whose
blood had been shed like water, began upon earth,
and Christ and His Vicar raised aloft the Cross triumphant over His enemies, proclaiming new laws of
chastity and charity. Great changes are effected in
the world insensibly and without effort. The work
of Providence is stately and slow, like the rising of a
deluge, and nothing is violent. To the eye of an
unbeliever, the progress of Christianity does little or
nothing, but to the eye of faith the transfiguration is
miraculous. The change in old Rome was in fact
marvellous, and its fall from its ancient glory and
terrible magnificence was a deadly wound to the
power of the prince of this world. In place of
the beast whose iron teeth had broken to pieces
the kingdoms of the earth and of the great statue
seen by Nebuchodonosor—the little stone descend-
ing from the mountain and crushing the giant
idol filled the earth—Constantine, who triumphed
under the Cross, raised it above the imperial crown,
and, acknowledging Christ to be his Master, yielded

9

the first place to Him, abandoning the old Rome to be the centre of the world and the seat of Peter, to shine henceforth as the light of all nations and the glory of the Christian people.

In St. Silvester's time some northern nation or nations were converted to the faith, and the names of Frumentius, Julianus, and Edisius are recorded as missioners to the heathen sent from Alexandria. The great St. Antony was famous for his sanctity, and St. Helena and Constantine recommended themselves to his prayers.

If all the sums expended by this great emperor in building churches could be calculated, they would exceed the expenditure of Solomon, for two millions of gold pieces are said to have been spent on the Church of St. Saviour alone ; and if to these sums are added the liberal gifts of land and tributes, there is little need of further question as to the donation of Constantine.   He gave the Church of Rome inde- · pendence, bestowing upon it a very large revenue. He did away with the power of the Prætorian Guard, and removed the seat of empire, leaving the Pope free, the uncontrolled master of large estates, whatever may have been the limits of them.   Not only Italy, but Greece, Africa and Asia are mentioned as contributing to the support of the Church of Rome.

To quote again the words of Sigonius : Constantine gave the Church " rich possessions of land."   He gave it freedom and a certain dominion, and not only in Rome, but throughout the world, he supported it liberally, acknowledging its authority, and has merited the title of Great, as a brave and wise emperor, and, it may be added, as good and holy prince, and well-deserving of the world. His laws bespeak a man of large and enlightened mind, and they changed the face of the civilised world, or rather formed the germ of its civilisation ; for so long as heathenism was dominant, with its idol-worship, its bacchanalian and blood-stained rites, its child-murder and uncontrolled licentiousness, its slavery and oppression, Europe could not be called civilised. Meekness and gentleness of manner, springing from charity, are the characteristics of true civilisation, and by his obedience to the Church and subordination to it, as representing the majesty of God, Constantine laid the foundations of the fabric of the Heavenly City, ruling in this world under the Vicar of Christ, to whom the proud powers of the earth are so unwilling to bow the head.

CHAPTER XII.

Two cities have been portrayed in the preceding pages, one rising and the other falling, side by side, the City of God and the mystical Babylon, the City of Confusion. The kingdom of Christ has been slowly rising out of the ruins of the fall of heathenism. It can hardly be imagined how appalling, and yet how seductive, the power of heathen superstition was before the reign of Christian principles began to prevail, though painted in some of its most revolting features by the pens of the heathen themselves, and but slightly veiled in the dubious and half-ironical praises of Gibbon.

Three features of the splendour of ancient Rome represent the principal allurements of old pagan life which was passing away, the baths, the amphi-theatres and the temples. A succession of emperors spent on these—but especially on the two first—incalculable sums, pandering to the luxury and passions of the people. It was a donative to the populace by which they won the name of munificent benefactors, and supplied the meanest citizen of Rome with the greatest of gratifications.

The Baths of Nero, Caracalla, the Antonines and Diocletian, and others which have been briefly mentioned, were open to the public for the fourth of a penny. The bathers were supplied with unguents, unless they preferred to bring with them more expensive perfumed ointments. Cold, or tepid, or hot and vapour baths were ready, and some took vapour baths of a very high temperature and then plunged in cold water. Before entering the bath or course of baths they stripped in public and took exercise in halls or porticoes : and round the bathing-rooms were gardens and porches or saloons in which poets declaimed and philosophers lectured. The immense fabric often covered a square of a thousand or two thousand feet, and was adorned within and without with costly marbles, paintings and statues. Some of the most famous ancient pieces of sculpture, such as the Farnese Hercules and the group of the Laocoon, have been found in the ruins of the baths. Theatres and temples were sometimes included in the building. The richest marble quarries in the world supplied the pillars, and the pavement and walls were beautifully decorated, so that nothing was wanting which luxury or magnificence could suggest.

The passion for bathing was great among the people, and laws were enacted that the baths should not be open before a certain hour, which was usually two in the afternoon, and should be closed before the evening fell, to avoid abuses. But, notwithstanding, great disorders are said to have taken place under the later emperors. In proportion to their evil propensities, the tyrants of Rome vied with each other in raising these costly edifices, and Christian confessors toiled in their construction. The last and most splendid were the Baths of Diocletian.

With Christianity a change came, and a new spirit breathed amid the corruption which had so universally prevailed. The publicity, the ornaments and accompaniments of the baths and their costly luxury were not agreeable to Christian modesty. This virtue, unknown or disregarded in heathen life, gradually leavened the public taste and manners, and the blood of Cecilia and Agnes and the virgin martyrs, with the devotion to the great Virgin Mother of God, gave birth to a veneration for chastity and honour of virginity. Old things passed away or were purified, as in the laver of a baptismal regeneration, and new things took their place by a solemn transformation as grace began to prevail. A higher and purer beauty, both in idea and in art, arose as stately churches in honour of the apostles and the martyrs were built, or ancient basilicas adapted to the usages of true religion. To the eyes of the infidel and the sceptic the scene which was dissolved may appear more agreeable, as it was more alluring, and Rome in the day of its triumph was grand with an earthly glory, but the Christian turns away instinctively from the contemplation of the old wickedness and sensuality of Paganism, to the humbler, but purer, spectacle of the gospel virtues leavening the corruption of mankind, and the mystical City of God building not for time, but for eternity.

The second great feature of heathen life and manners is represented by the amphitheatres. In

these the pomp and magnificence of the Pagan holiday
was chiefly displayed. The cost of the Coliseum was
something fabulous, and would have sufficed to build
a large capital city. According to Dion, nine thousand wild beasts were exhibited in the hunts or shows
at its dedication. A thousand ostriches, a thousand
deer or antelopes and a thousand wild-boars were
turned into the arena at once by Probus, and the
emperors vied with each other in their exhibitions of
strange or savage beasts, by which they gained the
fame of munificence and won popularity. Heliogabalus earned contempt and derision by a show of
thousands of mice and weasels. The emperors sat
in state on the suggestus, that is under a canopy on
the podium or platform immediately above the arena,
to preside at the games. Scented liquids were
scattered profusely over the assembly through concealed conduits, and awnings were extended above
to screen the whole audience from the heat of the
sun, supported by masts fixed in rings round the
circumference of the theatre and managed by sailors.
The difficulty of extending these curtains over so
vast a surface and managing them in a wind when
extended, has given rise to much discussion, and
Lucretius compares the rattling of them shaken by
the blast to a thunderstorm.

Sometimes beasts fought with beasts, elephants
with tigers, panthers, or lions, and sometimes men
contended with them, as in the modern bull-fight,
armed with a sword and a veil to throw over the
eyes of the animal. But the favourite entertain-
ment was the inhuman sport of matching gladiators

in pairs, and these were numerous in proportion to the solemnity of the show. We see in the pictures or frescoes which have been exhumed at Pompeii that sometimes horsemen in full armour, like medieval suits, fought with shield and lance. The Thracian, or Samnite, so called from his buckler and fashion of accoutrements, contended with a Gaul, or myrmillo, in a hideous mask or helmet with closed visor. The retiarius, who carried a net to throw over his adversary, and a trident, or three-pronged spear, was matched with a man-at-arms. These trained gladiators were kept by the masters or lanistæ in great numbers, and were at times, from their force and desperation, causes of alarm to Rome. On more than one occasion they broke out and stood for their lives against the soldiery, as it mattered little to them how they were butchered. They were usually bound by an oath to fight for the glory and die in obedience to the laws of the arena. Such were the amusements of the people and even of the matrons of Rome.

The appetite for blood engendered by these frightful exhibitions required to be fed, and was from time to time satiated with the slaughter of Christians; and the people, accustomed to it, saw with unconcern the death of the martyrs, torn to pieces by lions or tossed by bulls, though they wondered at their strange intrepidity, or, as they termed it, insensibility. By an Edict of Constantine, the shedding of human blood in the theatres was forbidden, and the hateful custom ceased. The faction fights of the race-course of Constantinople for the several colours of the white, red, and blue, were the last remnants of the ancient games.

This again was an extraordinary change wrought by Christianity, and an instance of the transforming power of the true religion. By degrees slavery was eliminated with its barbarities. Livy relates the story of a poor slave driven with blows across the circus before the games began, under the fork, that is, with the heavy instrument of torture on his neck, and that the festival was declared by the augurs to be polluted.

In the " Odyssey," when Ulysses comes home, he hears late at night the sigh of the feeble female slave, having accomplished her task of grinding at the mill ; and since the days of the Pharaohs of Egypt this melancholy lot had been the condition of an immense portion of mankind. In imperial Rome the labour of life was chiefly done in the slave-factories or prison-houses, and one master would be the possessor of tens of thousands of these captives. Christianity gradually did away with the inequality of men and nations, and the hard indifference to human life and suffering which characterised heathenism, for it created ties of affection between man and man hitherto unknown. But it raised up especially the domestic union of the family, giving to woman and to the mother her place and her respect. The pleasures of the heathen were public, they had no home ; they lived in the baths, in the theatre, in the forum. Except for the banquet, they spent little of the day at their houses. Hence the importance attached to these public places of amuse-

ment—the baths and amphitheatres.   Christianity,
by creating charity and human sympathy, and by
cementing the family, opened new pleasures which
overcame and expelled the selfish customs of the
past.   The creation of the family home is eminently
Christian, and the source of the happiness of nations
is the lesson of charity and mutual forbearance learned
at the domestic hearth.

The third great charm of heathen life was its
mythology, with its poetry, peopling the earth and
sea as well as Olympus, and its hero worship, the
beauty of its temples and the splendour of its religious
rites and festivals.   Greece had moulded statues to
represent the Jove of Homer, with ambrosial locks,
and Apollo as when he descended to loose his arrows
on the camp, or slay the Python.   Diana and Cytherea
lived in marble, and grottoes and groves had their
nymphs and naiads.   Hero-worship exercised a
powerful influence, especially in the localities where
the mighty dead were honoured.   In a writer of
the second century we find sailors attributing a
storm at sea to their neglect in honouring Ulysses
as they passed Ithaca.   The same author describes
a procession or embassy of youths and maidens to
Delphi, bringing a hecatomb in honour of Neopto-
lemus.   It is worth transcribing for its testimony to
the prevalence of hero-worship alluded to so frequently in the pages of Herodotus, as well as for the
description of a religious procession bringing a hecatomb for sacrifice.

" First came the hecatomb, conducted by men
initiated in the sacred mysteries, habited in a simple

rustic garb. Their white tunics were gathered up with a belt, leaving the right breast and arm and shoulder bare. In their hands they bore a battle-axe with a double blade. The bulls were all black, curving their necks, which were slightly arched, and with even straight horns, partly gilded and partly wreathed with flowers, crook-kneed, and with dew-laps hanging down to their knees. They were exactly a hundred, and other victims of different kinds followed, each in order and in droves apart, conducted with music of pipes and flutes, playing a prelude to the sacrifice. Then followed a company of Thessalian maidens, clad in beautiful embroidered tunics, with broad girdles and loose-flowing hair. They were divided into two choirs, one of which carried baskets full of flowers and fruits, and the other baskets of sweetmeats and fragrant spices, which filled the air with sweet odours. They made no use of their hands to carry these, but balancing them upon their heads, danced in order, hand in hand, going on in procession as they danced, while one choir sang, the other joining in the refrain."

Then follows the hymn sung in praise of Neopto-lemus, son of the great Achilles, and grandson of Thetis, praying him to be propitious and to avert evils.

"The melody was so sweet, and the time they kept with the beating of their feet so exact, that the pleasure of the ear surpassed that of the spectacle, and the crowd of lookers on were entranced, as they gazed and followed with their eyes the maidens as they passed along, until their attention was drawn away by the troop that followed of young men on horseback, and the chief of the embassy appeared, showing a sight surpassing all that could delight the ear. The troop of youths was fifty in number, twenty-five on each side of their leader, forming his bodyguard. Their buskins were laced with purple thongs, and their white mantles, clasped with buttons of gold, were bordered on the edge with blue. Every horse was from Thessaly, with the free look of its wide plains, champing at the bit disdainfully, as if they needed no such reminder to obey the rider. They were so covered with ornamental trappings, and decked with frontlets of gold and silver, that each seemed to vie with the other in splendid furniture.

" The leader" (of the race of Neoptolemus) "eclipsed the rest; like them, he was on horseback and in armour, carrying a lance of ash-tree wood with a cusp of bronze. His head was unhelmeted, and his scarlet mantle, embroidered with gold, represented the battle of the Centaurs and Lapithæ. Its morse or clasp was an amber Pallas, having on her shield the Gorgon's head."

The work of Heliodorus, of Tricca, in Thessaly, from which this is taken, contains much to illustrate the splendour of religious worship, especially in honour of Phœbus and Diana. He was a native of Emesa, and of the royal family of the priests of the sun, and hence the frequency of his mention of Apollo. Afterwards, as a Christian, he was required to burn his work, probably as painting heathenism in too favourable a light.

The tendency of Paganism was to deify Nature, and to increase the love of this life with its fleeting pleasures. Thus the odes of Horace are full of thoughts upon the enjoyments of the present hour; to make the most of them, because they cannot last long, and when youth is past and age is come, there remains nothing but the tomb. The cypress alone will weep over the sepulchre and follow its master, therefore the rose must be gathered while it blooms; brief life must be enjoyed, for then the three sisters cut the web, the poor ghost will depart to the shades, and all must go where Tullus and Ancus are gone. The melancholy thought that death ends all is made use of to enhance the necessity of making the most of the present, as the Egyptians of old carried round the banquet-hall the bodies of the dead, to exhort the guests to be merry while life lasts. Man bids farewell to life for ever, the envious gods alone enjoy happy immortality. Such was the thought of the Pagan.

It is obvious how much this hopeless and dreary prospect must have increased the eagerness for the goods of the present life, and this was the petition of the heathen, that the gods would avert the evils of the present and give them long and pleasant days. It is needless to dwell on the morality engendered by such thoughts, and by the very names of the deities, the objects of worship. The Epistle of St. Paul to the Romans gives a summary of the state of the heathen, and the " Satires " of Juvenal and "History" of Tacitus are a comment upon the catalogue of their sins. " Who," exclaims the satirist, " in such times of depravity could abstain from invective ?" Hero-worship itself, which in former times was paid to the noble or renowned, degenerated into the worship of Antinous, the favourite of Hadrian.

But another odious feature, less spoken of, but not less practised, was the use of magic and enchantment, common amongst the vulgar, as appears from the tale of Lucian. Heliodorus describes the method of practising necromancy or inquiry from the dead, with horrible rites performed over a corpse by a professor of the art, and Horace has allusions as to the prevalence of witchcraft. The emperors themselves, Maxentius, Maximinus Macrinus, and others, inquired into the future by divination, not only from the entrails of victims, but from slaughtered infants. Idolatrous superstition is seldom or never free from dealing with the devil, and Julian, when he endeavoured to restore Paganism, studied and practised the arts of magic.

Into Rome, as a centre, flowed all the superstitions of the world, of the Phrygian Cybele, the Egyptian Isis, of the Phœnician worship of the sun and the mythology of Greece. The empire, as it embraced, admitted the gods of every nation, and adopted every form of error ; but all alike tended to encourage a love of this life and a horror of death, excepting alone the death of the renowned of old and a glorious sepulchre. But this had long sunk into oblivion, and the general state of society was a professed seeking of sensual enjoyment as long as the gods permitted life to last, and the dreaded Proserpine and fatal sisters allowed the thread of allotted days to be spun unbroken.

When St. Paul preached at the Areopagus, his announcement of the resurrection of the body and a life to come was received with derision by the sages of Athens, but some believed. The preaching of Christianity is the preaching of the resurrection—of judgment and life to come. Of this the Catacombs are full; the paintings for the most part represent the vivifying power of grace, the restoration of Lazarus to life, the rising of Jonas from the jaws of death, Noah delivered from the deluge and Daniel from the lions, bespeaking the language of hope. Instead of the old inscriptions on the tomb " Farewell for ever"—" In æternum vale "—we read in the cemeteries, " Innocent soul, refreshed in Christ, pray for us !" " In light and peace, pray for us."

This truth once established in the soul, the joys of the present life, which so quickly pass away, and of which the heathen poet complained that even in the very moment of gratification there is something in the height of them which embitters, become in comparison of little worth, and its pains for the sake of future joys not only endurable, but desirable. This thought kept Lawrence firm upon the coals, and filled the martyrs with hope and joy. It is the groundwork of the faith, as St. Paul proclaims, " For if the dead rise not," he says, " our faith is vain." " Let us eat and drink, for to-morrow we die," thus summing up the principle of Christian life and the despairing doctrine of the heathen.

When the cry arose in the Ulpian Basilica, " Let the temples be closed, Christ is the true God," the Church of the Catacombs, after three centuries of

blood and oppression, came forth triumphant over
superstition and idolatry, and the laws of Constantine
established, together with the worship of the true
God, the law of Christian charity, and liberty to the
slave, and the law of chastity and conjugal fidelity.
To dissolve these is to return to heathenism and its
corruptions, for if the bond of marriage is broken, the
worst kind of licence prevails, and society is wounded
and poisoned at its source ; if charity, founded on
the unity of faith, is banished to make room for a
hollow philanthropy, the body politic becomes a
cloak for mutual aggression, until it ends in a reign
of terror ; and if truth ceases to be the basis of
religion and every man makes gods of his own or
worships none, a double darkness descends upon the
earth, for in Pagan times the God of Nature had at
least a semblance of honour, while modern impiety,
having rejected grace, cannot return to natural sim-
plicity.

It may seem that the change under Constantine is
pictured in rosy colours, and that his coins, as well
as some historians, present him in a more unfavourable light. The absence of Christian emblems on
his coins is no positive proof, nor is tradition to be
thrown aside because opposed by enemies of Catholicity. It is not said that in his earlier reign he
openly avowed or acknowledged the truth of Christianity, but, after his promulgation of the laws which
he issued from the Ulpian Basilica, he became the
public protector of the faith and worship of Christ,
and his triumphal arch accords with the Catholic
tradition.

APPENDIX I.

ON THE CARDINALS.

ALTHOUGH the "*name*" of the cardinal bishops, priests and deacons of the Holy Roman Church was not given from the very first, but came in progress of time, nevertheless the office existed from the beginning, attached to the Pontificate, the duties of which could not be adequately fulfilled without the assistance, counsel and ministry of many subordinate officials. Such were Linus, Cletus, Clement, Anacletus, and Mark the Evangelist in the time of St. Peter, and others, who were his coadjutors and counsellors. Pope Evaristus divided the city into parishes with titles or parochial endowments, and Hyginus assigned to the clergy the order of their rank. The seven deacons were appointed to the care of the seven regions of the city shortly after the times of Nero, and in the time of St. Silvester the names of the seven given in the Council of Rome held in the Baths of Domitian were, Fabianus, Marcus, Liberius, Arcidamus, Julius, Priscus, and Theodorus.

The Roman Church was very soon enriched by the contributions and legacies of pious men and women. These afforded support to the titles or parish churches

10

to which the cardinal priests were attached. Such were
the ancient titles of Equitius, Vestina, Pammachius,
Lucina, Julius, Callixtus, Eudoxia, Damasus, Pastor,
Emiliana, Crescentiana, Fasciola, and Tigridis. When
the revenues from the villas or farms or moneys attached were abundant, two or three cardinal priests
were appointed to a title. For instance, three subscribe
themselves of the title of Julius—Paulus, Marcellinus,
and Septimius ; three of the title of Equitius—Felix,
Sebastianus, and Adeodatus ; two of Marcellus—
Timotheus and Venantius ; and this was the manner
of signature in the persecuting times ; but when
public churches were opened, after the time of St.
Silvester, the church was named, as well as the title,
and the signature in full was, for example, Laurence,
cardinal priest of Silvester in Esquiliæ, under the
title of Equitius ; John, cardinal priest of SS. Vitalis, Gervase, and Protase, under the title of Vestina ;
Andromachus, cardinal priest of St. Peter ad Vincula,
under the title of Eudoxia.

The number of the cardinals, unless the words of
Pope Anacletus are to be understood to restrict them
to seventy-two, is not defined. He says "that the
seventy-two disciples elected by the Apostles are a
type of the Presbytery, and that they are represented
by it in the constitution of the Church." The number
varied at various times. In the Pontificate of
Pius IV. there were seventy-six ; in that of
Paschal II., ninety. In the time of Innocent II.
and Celestine II. there were only forty ; from Boniface VIII. to Sixtus IV., only thirty. They were increased to fifty under Alexander VI., to sixty-two

under Leo X., and to seventy-six under Paul III., Paul IV., and Gregory XIII. Sixtus V. had seventy.

The twenty-eight most ancient titles are thus given by Anastasius the librarian :

1. Sti. Julii, alias Sti. Callixti, alias Stæ. Mariæ Trans Tiberim.
2. Sti. Chrysogoni, trans Tiberim.
3. Stæ. Cæciliæ trans Tiberim.
4. Stæ. Anastasiæ sub Palatio.
5. Sti. Damasi, alias S. Laurentii in Damaso.
6. Sti. Marci ad Palatinas.
7. Sti. Equitii, alias Sti. Silvestri vel Sti. Martini in Montibus.
8. Stæ. Sabinæ in Aventino.
9. Stæ. Priscæ in Monte Aventino, alias SS. Aquilæ et Priscæ.
10. Stæ. Crescentianæ.
11. Fasciolæ, alias SS. Nerei et Achilli.
12. Sti. Caii.
13. Lucinæ secundæ, seu S. Marcelli.
14. S. Susannæ ad duas domos, alias S. Gabinii et Susannæ.
15. XII. Apostolorum, alias SS. App. Philippi et Jacobi.
16. Sti. Cyriaci in Thermis Diocletiani.
17. Sti. Eusebii.
18. Sti. Pastoris, alias Sti. Pudentis vel Pudentianæ.
19. Vestinæ, seu SS. Gervasii et Portasii vel Sti. Vitalis.
20. Sti. Matthæi in Merulana.
21. Sti. Clementis.
22. Stæ. Praxedis.

23. Sti. Petri ad Vincula vel Eudoxiæ.
24. Lucinæ vel Sti. Laurentii in Lucina.
25. Stæ. Æmilianæ.
26. Sti. Nicomedis.
27. Pammachii, alias SS. Joannis et Pauli.
28. Tigridis, alias Sti. Sixti.

Five of these were changed by St. Gregory I., and instead of the titles—

1. Stæ. Crescentianæ,
2. Sti. Nicomedis,
3. Sti. Caii,
4. Stæ. Æmilianæ,
5. Sti. Matthæi in Merulana,

were substituted the five following, namely,

1. Stæ. Balbinæ in Aventino,
2. SS. Petri et Marcellini,
3. Stæ. Crucis in Jerusalem,
4. Sti. Stephani in Monte Cœlio,
5. SS. Quatuor Coronatorum.

Sixtus IV. added a new title of St. Nicolas near the Colosseum, and Leo X. restored the ancient title of St. Matthew in Merulana, adding nine others in the year 1477 :

1. Sti. Joannis ante Portam Latonam,
2. Stæ. Agnetis in Agone,
3. Sti. Apollinaris,
4. Sti. Laurentii in pane et pernâ,
5. Sti. Silvestri in Campo Martio,
6. Sti. Thomæ in Parione,
7. Sti. Pancratii,
8. Sti. Bartholomæi in insulâ,
9. Stæ. Mariæ in Capitolio, seu Ara Cœli.

Paul IV., in the year 1557, erected the new title of St. Mary Super Minervam ; and Sixtus V., suppressing some of the ancient, added ten titles :

1. SSæ. Trinitatis in Monte Pincio,
2. Sti. Salvatoris in Lauro,
3. Stæ. Mariæ de Populo,
4. Stæ. Mariæ de Pace,
5. Stæ. Mariæ trans Pontem,
6. Sti. Petri in Montorio,
7. Sti. Augustini,
8. Sti. Blasii de Annulo,
9. Sti. Alexii in Aventino,
10. Sti. Onuphrii in Vaticano.

Pauvini gives the following list of the cardinals and their titles in the time of Pope Gelasius, A.D. 494 :

1. Cælius Laurentius, Presb. Card. in tit. Stæ. Praxedis. Stæ. R. E. Archipresbyter.
2. Martianus, Presb. Card. in tit. Stæ. Cæciliæ trans. Tiberim.
3. Cælius Januarius, Presb. Card. SS. Vitalis, Gervasii et Protasii, in tit. Vestinæ.
4. Gordianus, Presb. Card. SS. Joannis et Pauli, in tit. Pammachii.
5. Petrus, Presb. Card. in tit. Sti. Xti. Martyris Clementis in Monte Cœlio.
6. Paulinus, Presb. Card. Sti. Mariæ trans Tiberim, in tit. Callixti et Julii.
7. Valens, Presb. Card. in tit. Sti. Sabinæ in Monte Aventino.
8. Petrus, Presb. Card. in tit. Sti. Chrysogoni trans Tiberim.

9. Asterius, Presb. Card. SS. Pudentis et Pudentianæ, in tit. Pastoris.
10. Felix, Presb. Card. Sti. Silvestri in Esquiliis, in tit. Equitii.
11. Projectitius, Presb. Card. Sti. Laurentii Ms. in tit. Sti. Damasi.
12. Jovinus, Presb. Card. tit. Stæ. Xti. Virginis et Martyris Æmilianæ.
13. Bonus, Presb. Card. in tit. Stæ. Crescentianæ.
14. Probianus, Presb. Card. in tit. Sti. Eusebii in Esquiliis.
15. Sebastianus, Presb. Card. in tit. Sti. Xti. Martyris Nicomedis.
16. Martianus, Presb. Card. in tit. Sti. Cyriaci in Thermis Diocletiani.
17. Andreas, Presb. Card. in tit. Sti. Ap. et Evang. Matthæi.
18. Romanus, Presb. Card. in tit. Tigride.
19. Marcellus, Presb. Card. in tit. Sti. Stephani in Monte Cœlio.
20. Asellus, Presb. Card. tit. SS. Gabinii et Susannæ ad duas domos.
21. Anastasius, Presb. Card. in tit. Stæ. Xti. Virg. et Mart. Anastasiæ.
22. Epiphanius, Presb. Card. in tit. SS. XII. Apostolorum.
23. Acontius, Presb. Card, in tit. Fasciolæ.
24. Benedictus, Presb. Card. in tit. Sti. Caii.
25. Dominicus, Presb. Card. in tit. SS. Aquilæ et Priscæ in Monte Aventino.
26. Stephanus, Presb. Card. in Sti. Xti. Mart. Marcelli.

27. Epiphanius, Presb. Card. in tit. Sti. Evang. Marci.

28. Hilarius, Presb. Card. Sti. Laurentii, Mart. in tit. Lucinæ.

Then follows a list of the archpriests, of the titles, twenty-four in number, and eleven minor priests, after which is a list of the cardinal deacons :

DIACONI CARDINALES VII.

Cyprianus, S. R. E. Archidiaconus et in Regione III^a et X^a Diac. Card.

Anastasius, Diac. Card. in Regione IV^a et XI^a

Tarrensis, Diac. Card. in Regione I^a et VIII^a

Citonatus, Diac. Card. in Regione V^a et XII^a

Tertullius, Diac. Card. in Regione VI^a et XIII^a

Joannes, Diac. Card. in Regione II^a et IX^a

Cælius Joannes, Diac. Card. in Regione VII^a et XIV^a

"By the constitution of Sixtus V.," says Fr. Oldoin, "the number of cardinals was determined to seventy, of which fifty were priests, fourteen deacons, and six bishops."

The cardinal priests were reckoned first, and after the cardinal priests the deacons, who at first were seven, and afterwards fourteen, to whom four deacons of the palace were added by Gregory III., so that at one time there were eighteen, with the following titles :

S. Mariæ in Dominica.

Sti. Lucæ in Circo.

Stæ. Mariæ Novæ.

SS. Cosmæ et Damiani.

Sti. Hadriani.

SS. Sergii et Bacchi.

Sti. Theodori.

Sti. Georgii in Velabro.

Stæ. Mariæ in Cosmedin.

Stæ. Mariæ in Porticu.

Sti. Nicolai in Carcere Tulliano.

Sti. Angeli in Piscina.

Sti. Eustachii juxta Pantheon.

Stæ. Mariæ in Aquiro.

Stæ. Mariæ in Viâ Lata.

Stæ. Agathæ in Equo Marmoreo.

Stæ. Mariæ in Silicæ, alias Caput Suburræ.

SS. Viti et Modesti in Macello Martyrum.

The four deacons of the palace were not long retained, but were made cardinal priests.

The cardinal bishops were the last in order of creation, and though they have varied somewhat in number under various Popes, were generally seven, assistant bishops of the Lateran Basilica, with titles from neighbouring cities or states :

1. The Cardinal Bishop of Ostia.
2. The Cardinal Bishop of SS. Ruffina and Secunda, or of Silva Candida.
3. The Cardinal Bishop entitled Portuensis.
4. The Cardinal Bishop of Sabinum.
5. The Cardinal Bishop of Præneste.
6. The Cardinal Bishop of Tusculum.
7. The Cardinal Bishop of Albano.

APPENDIX II.

THE CATACOMBS.—THEIR NAMES AND LOCALITIES.

FIFTY cemeteries, more or less, for some reckon sixty, may be counted in subterranean Rome. The most ancient is the Cemetery of St. Peter, or the Vatican. Next to it, on the Aurelian Road, is that of SS. Processus and Martinian, with those of St. Calepodius, St. Julius, and St. Agatha. The Cornelian Road branches from the Aurelian, and though celebrated for the martyrdom of SS. Rufina and Secunda, has no cemetery upon it. These two roads run in a westerly direction from the Vatican. The Portuan Way runs south-east, and on it are the Catacombs of St. Felix, St. Pontian, and St. Generosa.

On the other side of the Tiber the Ostian Way has the Cemeteries of St. Paul, St. Timothy, and St. Felix and Adauctus, of St. Cyriacus and St. Zenon running in a southerly direction, as seen from the Vatican. Beyond it, in the same direction on the road to Ardea, which is a branch from the Appian, are the Cemeteries of St. Flavia Domitilla, SS. Nereus and Achilles, SS. Marcus and Marcellianus, St. Balbina and St. Mark. This is the most populous part of the subterranean city, for here the Appian

Road has the Cemetery of St. Callixtus, and those of St. Zephyrinus, St. Prætextatus, St. Soter, and SS. Eusebius and Marcellus, which extend far away to St. Paul's.

More easterly, on the Latin Road, near St. John's, are the Cemeteries of SS. Gordian and Epimachus, SS. Simplician and Servilian, and on the Lavicanian Way the Cemeteries of St. Tibertius, SS. Marcellinus and Peter, with that of St. Helena, and of SS. Claudius and Nicostratus. To the east, on the Tiburtine Road, which runs to Tivoli, are the Catacombs of St. Lawrence and St. Cyriaca, of great extent. To the north-east, out of the Porta Pia, on the Nomentan Road, are the Cemeteries of St. Nicomedes, St. Alexander, SS. Primus and Felician, and of St. Agnes.

More towards the north, on the Salarian Way, lie the Catacombs of St. Priscilla, SS. Chrysanthus and Darius, St. Silvester, St. Felicitas, and St. Alexander; and on the old Salarian Way that of St. Hermes. Lastly, to the north-west, on the Flaminian Way, are the Cemeteries of SS. Valentine, Julius, and Theodora.

It is calculated that the catacombs would form a street three hundred leagues long, with six million tombs of the dead. They are cut in the granular tufo, which is sufficiently hard to support the shelves and form the galleries, while it is soft enough to be easily worked. They are entirely the work of Christians.

The bodies enclosed in the niches or shelves in the sides of the galleries were often wrapped in linen, with spices and aromatic gums, the odour of which was sometimes sensible when they were opened. The fossors employed under the seven regionary deacons were an order occupied in the work of excavation and burial. Sometimes when it was difficult or dangerous to carry out the debris, the galleries already used seem to have been filled, or partially filled again.

In the Cemetery of the Vatican a great number of Popes were buried, and afterwards of kings and emperors. The Cemetery of St. Calepodius, though probably of a more ancient date, is named from the martyred priest in the time of the Emperor Alexander, who was dragged through the streets of Rome and thrown into the Tiber, from which his body was recovered and buried by Pope Callixtus.

The Cemetery of SS. Processus and Martinian, the gaolers of St. Peter, in the Mamertine, is the most ancient, next to the Vatican, on the Aurelian Way, and between it and the Portuan Way is the Petra Scelerata, or stone of malefactors, on which were laid the four martyrs, Eusebius, Vincent, Peregrinus, and Pontian, in the time of Commodus, to be beaten to death. On the Cornelian Way, Rufina and Secunda have left their memories, who for their virginity suffered great torments, and were carried on that road to the Silva Nigra and there left dead. In the following night they appeared in a vision to Plautilla, a noble Roman lady of their acquaintance, and said, " Plautilla, cease to defile thyself with the worship of idols, and believe in Christ. Go to thy estate on the Cornelian Way, and thou wilt

find our bodies ; give them burial as thou canst."
She obeyed and believed, and from Silva Nigra the
name was changed to Silva Candida, one of the titles
of the cardinal bishops.

The cemetery on the Portuan Way is called from
St. Pontian, a noble Roman, who concealed St.
Callixtus in his house, and assisted him in the burial
of Calepodius. It is also called the Cemetery of
SS. Abdon and Sennen, Persian princes martyred
in the Amphitheatre in the time of Decius, and
buried there. The Catacomb of Generosa, near that
of St. Pontian, is probably named from some noble
lady, who, like the Lucinas—for there seem to have
been more than one of that name—gave her gardens
for burial.

The Cemetery of St.Timothy, on the Ostian Road,
is named from a noble citizen of Antioch, who came
to Rome in the time of Pope Melchiades, and from
a zealous heathen became a convert and preacher of
the faith. Tarquinius, the prefect of Maxentius,
seized him and threw him into a dungeon, and
besides other tortures, put him into burning lime.
He was buried by the Pope, assisted by St. Silvester, and the lady Theodora laid the body in a
garden near the Cemetery of St. Lucina.

In the Benedictine cloisters of St. Paul's there is
this ancient inscription : " Under this altar rest the
glorious bodies of the Apostles Peter and Paul (that
is to say, a portion of them, for the other portion is
laid in the Church of St. Peter), but their heads in
the Lateran ;" and a stone is preserved on which is
inscribed, " On this table of porphyry the bones of

the holy Apostles Peter and Paul were divided and weighed by the Blessed Silvester, Pope, in the year three hundred and nineteen, when this church was built."

The Cemetery of St. Cyriacus is named from the deacon, who, like St. Lawrence, was laid on the rack until all his bones were dislocated and then scalded with boiling pitch in the time of Maximian. Largus and Smaragdus and twenty soldiers suffered with him.

The Cemetery of Flavia Domitilla, on the road to Ardea, also called of St. Petronilla, dates from the Apostolic age. The daughter of St. Peter, or, as some say, his spiritual daughter Petronilla, was buried there, and afterwards Flavia Domitilla, niece of Titus and Domitian, who vowed virginity in the time of St. Clement. She was banished to the isle of Pontia, and, on her return, burned alive in her house with her two maidens Euphrosyna and Theodora at Terracina, from whence the bodies were brought to Rome by Auspicius, and buried in the crypt on her estate. Her two faithful martyred servants, SS. Nereus and Achilles, give their name to the same cemetery.

Between the road to Ardea and the Cemetery of St. Callixtus, on the Appian Way, extends the Cemetery of SS. Marcus and Marcellianus, two brothers condemned by the Prætor Fabianus in the great persecution under Diocletian. They were nailed to a tree, and their bodies pinned to it with javelins or lance-heads in every limb, until the prætor said, " Unhappy men, relent and be delivered from your torments!" And they replied, "Never was feast more delicious than the pains we endure for Christ. We are now fixed secure in His love." They were encouraged by St. Sebastian. The adjacent Cemetery of Balbina is named from the daughter of a tribune Quirinus, who was cured by kissing the chains of Hermes, the prefect of the city, converted by Pope Alexander. She devoted herself, like Lucina, to the burial of the martyrs. The Pope St. Mark built a church over the catacomb, and was himself buried there. On the Appian Road is the Cemetery of St. Callixtus. The entrance to this great cemetery is ordinarily made from the basilica of St. Sebastian. Here amidst innumerable martyrs were laid the bodies of Pope Anicetus, Anteros, Pontian, Fabian, Cornelius, Lucius, Stephen, Sixtus II., Dionysius, Eutychian, Eusebius, and Melchiades. The body of Sebastian, recovered from the sewer into which it had been cast, was buried in the Cemetery of St. Callixtus. A portion of the cemetery received its name from St. Cæcilia, and another portion from St. Sixtus. In this catacomb the arcosolium or arched tomb is more frequent, which is at the extremity of a chamber or cubiculum, and when the chamber was designed to form a chapel, the arched tomb was usually over the body of some great martyr.

The Catacomb of Prætextatus is one of the most ancient and extensive of the cemeteries. It contains some of the largest crypts and galleries, which seem to have served as a place of refuge. St. Prætextatus suffered martyrdom in the great persecution, having first been condemned to the mines. St. Sotera, martyred in the same persecution by Maximian, was a noble Roman virgin, who offered her face to the blows of the executioners, and gives her name to a portion of the cemetery. Another portion is named from SS. Eusebius and Marcellus, priest and deacon of Pope Stephen, by whom Adrias and Paulina, with their children, were brought to baptism. They were seized by a cohort of sixty soldiers, sent to take them in the crypt, with Hippolytus, and martyred by Valerian.

St. Eugenia, the daughter of Philip, Prefect of Egypt, gives the name to a cemetery on the Latin Road. Appearing to her mother Claudia, after martyrdom, she said, " Rejoice, mother, for the Lord has brought me into the joys of heaven. You will come to me on the Lord's day that is at hand. Tell my brothers Avitus and Sergius to be faithful to the sign of the Cross, that they may come to partake of our happiness." In the same catacomb on the Latin Way, Pope St. Stephen buried the martyrs Sempronius, Exuperius, Olympius, and Theodulus in the persecution of Valerian. The Cemetery of SS. Simplicius and Servilian, at the second milestone on the Latin Way, is more ancient, and belongs to the time of Trajan. Converted by the example of Flavia Domitilla, they were put to death by Anianus, prefect of the city, and buried by the Christians in a garden two miles from the walls. Contiguous to that of St. Simplicius is the Cemetery of St. Tertullian, who suffered a dreadful martyrdom in the persecution of Valerian.

On the Lavicanian Way is the Cemetery of SS. Tiburtius and Marcellinus. Tiburtius was the son of Chromatius, a young noble of Rome of great beauty in the time of Pope Caius, in the persecution of Diocletian. Denounced by a false Christian, Torquatus, to the Prefect Fabianus, he was commanded to walk upon burning coals, which seemed to him like a bed of flowers, and then beheaded. Tiburtius appeared in a vision to Lucilla and Firmina, his relatives, and, accompanied by Marcellinus and Peter the exorcist, commanded them to bury in the cemetery beside him the martyrs of the Silva Candida, Rufina and Secunda.

Near this cemetery, on the Lavicanian Way, is the burial-place of the Empress St. Helena, mother of Constantine, who erected there, in honour of the martyrs and for the love of his mother, a basilica of which there exist some remains. The four saints called the Quatuor Coronati, and their five companions, Claudius, Nicostratus, Symphorian, Castorius, and Simplicius, the sculptors who refused to make idols, were buried in this catacomb by a Christian, named Nicodemus, who drew their bodies out of the Tiber. The four Coronati, Severus, Severianus, Carpophorus, and Victorinus, are said to have been buried in this catacomb by St. Sebastian and a holy priest, who was afterwards Pope St. Melchiades. Their bodies, thrown to the dogs at the statue of Esculapius, could not be got possession of until five days after their martyrdom. The Cemetery of St. Castulus forms a portion of the same catacomb. He was of the household of Diocletian, and concealed the martyrs until he was betrayed by the same false Christian Torquatus who betrayed Tiburtius. The galleries are very narrow and tortuous in this cemetery, as if for concealment.

The Campus or Ager Veranus, on the road to Tivoli, was given by Cyriaca as a Christian sepulchre, and the body of St. Lawrence was laid there. She suffered martyrdom when of advanced age, and gives the name to a portion of the cemetery. An immense number of martyrs were buried in the Cemetery of St. Lawrence, amongst whom were Hippolytus, Abundius, Justin, Tryphonius and Cyrillus. The youthful Cyrillus, cruelly martyred by Decius, was left a prey to the dogs, and buried by St. Justin.

On the Nomentan Way is the ancient Catacomb ad Nymphas, where Papias and Maurus were buried in the time of Diocletian. In the fifth year of the building of the baths, the prefect Laodicius, seated on the tribunal in the Flaminian Circus, interrogated these two Christian soldiers. " I know that you are Christians," said the judge. " Yes, we are." " Leave your error and adore the gods." " To adore them is to renounce everlasting life." " If you do not adore, your life will be short ; do as I tell you and you shall live." " Do sacrifice yourself, and you will live in everlasting fires."

A shower of blows upon them followed this reply. They continued to exclaim : " Christ, support Thy servants." They were beaten to death with scourges laden with balls of lead. Their bodies were buried by night, " ad Nymphas, where Peter baptised," on the Nomentan Road. On the same road is the Cata-

11

comb of Nicomedes, a martyred priest in the time of
Domitian, discovered burying the dead.

Also the Catacomb of the Pope Alexander is on the
Nomentan Way, put to death by the judge Aurelian
with Eventius and Theodulus.   Severina, the wife of
the judge, buried them in her villa at the seventh
milestone.   Beyond is the Cemetery of SS. Primus
and Felician, martyred in the time of Diocletian.
At the fourth mile is the Cemetery of St. Agnes.
Her extreme youth, beauty, and courage have made
her name one of the most famous among the army of
martyrs.   In this catacomb the primitive paintings
are remarkable for their beauty.

The Via Salaria to the north has the ancient Cemetery of St. Priscilla, venerable as the burial-place of
the house of Pudens the senator, and his daughters
Praxedes and Prudentiana.   The popes Marcellus
and Silvester were buried in this catacomb, and Pope
Marcellinus and his companions Claudius, Cyrinus,
and Antoninus, after having lain unburied for thirty-
five days, were laid there in a " cubiculum clarum,"
or vaulted chamber of more conspicuous size.

On the old Salarian Road is the Catacomb " ad
Clivum Cucumeris," where, in the time of Claudius,
when the edict was given out that the Christians in
prison should be despatched without further inquiry,
two hundred and sixty Christians employed in the
sand-pits on the Via Salaria were shot to death with
arrows by soldiers, and their bodies thrown to be
burned on a great pyre, from which some were
snatched by Marius and Martha, with their sons Audifax and Abacuc or Abacum, a Christian pilgrim

from the East, and buried in this cemetery. Forty-six soldiers were martyred for having received baptism in the year 269, and buried by the priests John and Justin, " ad Clivum Cucumeris," and in the persecution of Diocletian a thousand soldiers, with their captain, Maximus, were martyred and buried in this cemetery.

The Cemetery of Theodora, on the Flaminian Way, completes the circuit of Rome. Here were laid the bodies of Abundius, priest, and Abundantius, deacon, who, on the way to martyrdom, restored to life the son of Marcius. By order of Diocletian, all were put to death, and they were buried with spices and aromatic gums by Theodora, at a distance from the city, on the Flaminian Way.

This *résumé* of the localities and chief names connected with the catacombs is taken from the work of the Abbé Gaume, entitled, " Les Trois Romes." It supplements and confirms the respective Lives of the Popes.

APPENDIX III.

THE discovery of the true Cross by St. Helena has given her celebrity in the annals of the Church, and throws a light upon the history of Constantine. After the victory over Maxentius, or when he became the master of the world, his mother went into the East to see the Cross under which her son had conquered. She discovered it by a miracle, and brought a portion to Rome, for the reception of which the Sessorian Basilica, otherwise called the Basilica of Helen, was built by Constantine, afterwards called St. Cross in Jerusalem, because a great quantity of earth from Calvary was placed in the chapel containing the holy relic.

Four massive golden candlesticks and fifty lamps of silver, five gold chalices and an altar of massive gold, were among the donations to the church, which have disappeared in the spoliations of Rome. But when the church—which was restored by St. Gregory II.—underwent alteration and renovation in the year 1492, the workmen discovered above the central arch, within the church, a hollow place, which, when it was opened, was found to contain a leaden case covered with a square marble slab, on which was written, " This is the title of the true Cross." Within the case was a little board, the edges of which were wasted by time, upon which was engraved, in letters painted red, " Jesus Judæorum Nazarenus rex," the word Judæorum partly gone from decay. The whole city ran to see it, and Pope Innocent himself came and ordered it to be kept in the case under a glass, and to be exposed only once a year on the festival of the church. St. Helena, following an ancient usage, had placed it in this elevated position when the church was built. In the chapel, which is dedicated to St. Helena, besides the portion of the Cross, are two thorns of the crown of thorns, and one of the nails with which Our Lord was crucified, and the sponge which was presented to Him dipped in gall.

The reverence which he paid his mother in building this basilica and the mausoleum, with a noble church, on the Lavicanian Way, shows the real disposition of Constantine. If his zeal for the Cross, after the miracle which gave him victory, seems to have languished for a time, it must be remembered that he succeeded to a Pagan empire and a Pagan senate. The arch of triumph erected by the senate and people bears witness at the same time to the truth of the miracle in ambiguous phrase, while it shows that as yet the senate would not acknowledge Christianity. The inscription says that " he conquered the tyrant, *instinctu divinitatis,*" but no cross is to be seen on the monument. Eusebius says that Constantine, not wishing to oppose the prejudices of the senate, out of policy did not take notice of it ; but that he erected in the city the cross on an obelisk, with an inscription that " Under this salutary sign I freed the senate and people of Rome from the yoke of tyranny." As to the argument drawn from coins of Constantine, it may be observed that the first Christian emperors on their medals and inscriptions have the Pagan title of "Pontifex Maximus," which in its original signification is " Builder of the Bridge." And Valentinian is so inscribed on the Bridge of Cestius. These remarks are extracted from the Abbé Gaume.

The vision of Constantine and the finding of the Holy Cross by St. Helena are unacceptable to the enemies of the Cross. Father Alford, in his " Ecclesiastical Annals," has an able dissertation on this subject, in which he gives the arguments to prove the British extraction of St. Helena.

The story of the Greek historian, Nicephorus, that St. Helena was the daughter of an innkeeper at Drepanum, is shown to be false, by the impossibility of reconciling it with chronology. He says that Constantinus Chlorus, on his embassy to the East, lodged in the house of an innkeeper at Drepanum, in Bithynia, and had a son by his daughter ; that on his return to Rome he was created Cæsar with Galerius, A.D. 292 ; that for fear of the jealousy of Theodora, he sent the boy Constantine to be brought up in the court of Nicomedia, where he was imbued with Christianity.

According to this story—improbable on account of the much-praised continence of Chlorus—Constantine would have been fourteen years old when he was proclaimed emperor, whereas he was thirty-three. His age shows that he was born when Chlorus was commander in Britain, to which he was sent in the time of the Emperor Aurelian. It is certain, moreover, that Maximian, when he required of Chlorus to marry his step-daughter, Theodora, demanded the divorce of Helena, and therefore she was the wife of Constantius. It is true that by the laws of Rome a man of senatorial rank in command of a province could not legitimately take a provincial to wife, unless he chose to do so after his office had expired. This may account for St. Helena being called by some the partner of Chlorus, but not his wife. She was, according to Eutropius and other historians, the daughter of a British prince who was the host of Constantius, or, as some say, the keeper of the horse, his stabularius, and hence the opprobrious name given to St. Helena of Stabularia. St. Ambrose in his sermon seems to attribute this reproach to the Jews, because she adorned the stable at Bethlehem.

Baronius thinks that Nicephorus may have confounded Britannia with Bithynia, and as Drepanum was called Helenopolis, and adorned by Constantine, have supposed it was the place of her birth.

By English historians she is said to have been born at Colchester, and the old arms of that city bore a cross in her memory. It is thought that Constantius Chlorus derived from her his goodwill to Christians, and it is said by some that he was converted before he died. The character of Con-

stantine, and especially his esteem of chastity, be-
tokens some early Christian impressions, and it is
a remarkable coincidence that the adoration of the
Cross, which was so special a characteristic of early
British Christianity, should have been spread in the
whole world by St. Helena and Constantine.

The holiness of St. Helena, venerated as a saint
by the Catholic Church, and the respect and love
borne to her by Constantine, is a sufficient refutation
of the calumnies of her enemies, and the silence of
Eusebius on subjects which give glory to Rome and
Catholicity is no argument, unless it be in her
favour.   She is styled in an ancient inscription,
" Venerabilis et piisima Augusta."

THE END.

R. WASHBOURNE, PRINTER, 18 PATERNOSTER ROW, LONDON.

NEW BOOKS.

Inner Life of Pere Lacordaire, O.P. From the French, by the author of "The Knights of St. John." New edition, revised, 6s. 6d.

Life of the Venerable Elizabeth Canori Mora. Translated from the Italian, with Preface by Lady Herbert. With Photograph, 3s. 6d.

Lives of the Early Popes. St. Peter to St. Silvester. By Rev. Thomas Meyrick, M.A. 8vo.

Tales of the Jewish Church. By Charles Walker. 12mo., 2s. 6d.

The Duties of Christian Parents. Conferences by Père Matignon. Translated by Lady Constance Bellingham, with Preface by Mgr. Capel, 12mo., 5s. *In the Press.*

Short Meditations, for every day in the Year. By an anonymous Italian author. Translated by Dom Edmund J. Luck, O.S.B. Prefaced by a letter of recommendation from His Eminence Cardinal Manning, 12mo. Edition for the Regular Clergy, 2 vols., 9s. Edition for the Secular Clergy, 2 vols., 9s.

Fr. Power's Catechism : Doctrinal, Moral, Historical, and Liturgical. Fourth Edition, enlarged, 3 vols., 10s. 6d.

The Rejection of Catholic Doctrines, attributable to the Non-Realization of Primary Truths. Exemplified in Letters to a Friend on Devotion to the B.V.M., the Angels, and Saints. By a Layman, 8vo., 1s.

On what Authority do I accept Christianity ? A Question for reasonable Members of the Church of England. 12mo., 6d.

Manual of Sacred Chant, containing the Ordinary of the Mass, the Psalms and Hymns of Vespers and Compline, &c., &c. Music and Words. By Rev. J. Mohr, S.J., 18mo., 2s. 6d.

Cantiones Sacrae. A Collection of Hymns and Devotional Chants for the different Seasons of the Year, &c., &c. Music and Words. By Rev. J. Mohr, S.J., 8vo., 5s.

. *Though this Catalogue does not contain many of the books of other Publishers, R. W. can supply any, no matter by whom they are published. All orders, so far as possible, will be executed the same day.*

School Books, *with the usual reduction,* Copy Books, and other Stationery, Rosaries, Medals, Crucifixes. Scapulars, Incense, Candlesticks, Vases, &c., &c., supplied.

Foreign Books supplied. The publications of the leading Publishers kept in stock. R. Washbourne's Catalogue of Books published in America, post free.

Life of the Rt. Rev. Dr. Dixon, Primate of all Ireland.
By Sister M. F. Clare. 8vo., 7s. 6d.

Manuel de Conversation.   12mo., 1s.

Allah Akbar—God is Great.   An Arab Legend of the Siege and
Conquest of Granada. From the Spanish. By Mariana Monteiro.
Contents :—1. The Genius of the Alhambra.   2. The King Abu-
Abd-Allah el Zogirbi.   3. Zegries and Abencerrajes.   4. The
Cypress . of the Sultana.   5. The Chamber of Lions.   6. The
Judgment of God.   7. Hernan Perez del Pulgar.   8. The Triumph
of the Ave Maria.   9. Gonzalo Fernandez de Cordova.   10. The
Conquest of Granada.   11. The Last Adieu.
Illustrated with Head Pieces from the pencil of Miss Henriqueta
Monteiro, and elaborately bound in accordance with the Arabic.
8vo., 3s. 6d.

The Fairy Ching ; or the Chinese Fairies' Visit to England.   By
Henrica Frederic.   12mo., cloth extra, 1s., gilt edges, 1s. 6d.

What Catholics do not Believe.   By the Right Rev. Bishop
Ryan, Coadjutor to the Archbishop of St. Louis.   12mo., 1s.

Life of Fr. Benvenuto Bambozzi, O.M.C., of the Conventual
Friars Minor.   Translated from the Italian (2nd Edition) of Fr.
Nicholas Treggiari, D.D.   12mo., 5s.   *In the Press.*

OREMUS, A Liturgical Prayer Book : with the Imprimatur
of the Cardinal Archbishop of Westminster.   An adaptation of the
Church Offices : containing Morning and Evening Devotions ;
Devotion for Mass, Confession, and Communion, and various other
Devotions ;   Common and Proper, Hymns, Lessons, Collects,
Epistles and Gospels for Sundays, Feasts, and Week Days ; and
short notices of over 200 Saints' Days.   Also short Liturgical
Devotions for Holy Week.   For greater convenience, the Latin has
been given of all the Psalms, Hymns, and other Prayers, occurring
in the ordinary services of the Church, in which the Faithful take
more or less part.   32mo., 452 pages, paper cover, 2s. ; cloth,
2s. 6d. ; embossed, red edges, 3s. 6d. ; French morocco, 4s. 6d. ;
calf, 5s. 6d. ; morocco, 6s.; Russia, 8s. 6d.   Also in superior or
more expensive bindings.

Are You Safe in the Church of England ?   A Question for
Anxious Ritualists.   By an Ex-Member of the Congregation of S.
Bartholomew, Brighton [Charles Walker].   8vo., 6d.

**Practical Hints on the Education of the Sons of Gentle-
men.**   By an Educator.   8vo., 1s.
Contents :—1. Introduction.   2. The Mind.   3. Preparatory Education.   4. The Existing System of Education.   5. How to Manage a
Class.   6. The Educator.   7. A Plea for the Study of Language.

The Child of Mary's Manual.   Compiled from the French.
Second Edition, with the Imprimatur of the Bishop of Clifton. 1s.

Gathered Gems from Spanish Authors.   By Mariana Monteiro, author of "The Monk of the Monastery of Yuste." 3s.

Life of St. Wenefred, Virgin Martyr and Abbess, Patroness of
North Wales and Shrewsbury.   By Rev. T. Meyrick, M.A. 2s.

A Catechism for First Confession. By the Rev. R. G. Davis. *Nihil Obstat :* Johannes Can. Crookall, S.T.D.,V.G. 32mo., 1d.

Stories of the Saints. By M. F. S. Saints of the Early Church. 12mo., 4th Series, 3s. 6d.; 5th Series, 3s. 6d.

The Holy Mass : The Sacrifice for the Living and the Dead. By Rev. M. Müller, C.SS.R. 12mo., 10s. 6d.

The Faith of our Fathers : Being a Plain Exposition and Vindication of the Church founded by our Lord Jesus Christ. By Most Rev. Archbishop Gibbons, 12mo. 4s. ; paper covers, 2s. nett.

ADELSTAN (Countess), Sketch of her Life and Letters, From the French of the Rev. Père Marquigny, S.J. 1s. & 2s. 6d.

Adolphus ; or, the Good Son. 18mo., 6d.

Adventures of a Protestant in Search of a Religion. By Iota. 12mo., 2s. and 3s. 6d.

AGNEW (Mme.), Convent Prize Book. 12mo., 3s. 6d.

A'KEMPIS—Following of Christ. Pocket Edition, 32mo., 1s.; embossed red edges, 1s. 6d.; roan, 2s.; French morocco, 2s. 6d.; calf or morocco, 4s. 6d.; gilt, 5s. 6d.; russia, with clasp, &c., 10s. 6d.; ivory, with rims and clasp, 15s., 16s., 18s.; morocco antique, with corners and clasps, 17s. 6d.; russia, ditto, ditto, 16s., 20s.

——— **Imitation of Christ ; with Reflections.** 32mo., 1s.; Persian calf, 3s. 6d.; 12mo., 3s. 6d.; mor., 10s. 6d.; mor. ant. 25s.

——— **The Three Tabernacles.** 16mo., 2s. 6d.

Albertus Magnus. *See* Dixon (Rev. Fr. T. A.).

Album of Christian Art. Twenty-three original composition Professor Klein, in Vienna. 4to., 7s. 6d.

Allah Akbar—God is Great. An Arab Legend of the Siege and Conquest of Granada. From the Spanish. By Mariana Monteiro. 12mo., 3s. 6d.

ALLIES (T. W.), St. Peter; his Name and his Office. 5s.

Alphabet of Scripture Subjects. On a large sheet, 1s.; coloured, 2s., mounted to fold in a book, 3s. 6d.

ALZOG'S Universal Church History. 8vo., Vols.i & ii, each 20s.

AMHERST (Rt. Rev. Dr.), Lenten Thoughts. 2s. 6d.

ANDERDON (Rev. W. H., S.J.), To Rome and Back. Fly-Leaves from a Flying Tour. 12mo., 2s.

ANDERSEN (Carl), Three Sketches of Life in Iceland. Translated by Myfanwy Fenton. 12mo., 2s. 6d.

Angela Merici (S.) Her Life, her Virtues, and her Institute. From the French of the Abbé G. Beetemé. 12mo., 4s. 6d.

Angela's (S.) Manual : a Book of Devout Prayers and Exercises for Female Youth. 2s.; Persian, 3s. 6d.; calf, 4s. 6d.

Angels (The) and the Sacraments. 16mo., 1s.

——— **Month of the Holy Angels.** By Abbé Ricard. 1s.

Angelus (The). A Monthly Magazine. 8vo., 1d. Yearly subscription, post free, 1s. 6d. Volume for 1876, cloth, 2s. 6d. 1877, 2s.

Anglican Orders. By Canon Williams. 12mo., 3s. 6d.

Anglicanism, Harmony of. *See* Marshall (T. W. M.).

Are You Safe in the Church of England? A Question for Anxious Ritualists. By an Ex-Member of the Congregation of S. Bartholomew, Brighton. 8vo., 6d.

ARNOLD (Miss M. J.), Personal Recollections of Cardinal Wiseman, with other Memories. 12mo., 2s. 6d.

ARRAS (Madame d') The Two Friends; or Marie's Self-Denial. 12mo., 1s.; gilt edges, 1s. 6d.

Ars Rhetorica. Auctore R. P. Martino du Cygne. 12mo., 3s.

Artist of Collingwood. 12mo.. 2s.

Association of Prayers. *See* Tondini (Rev. C.).

Augustine (St.) of Canterbury, Life of. 12mo., 3s. 6d.

Aunt Margaret's Little Neighbours; or, Chats about the Rosary. 12mo., 3s.

BAGSHAWE (Rev. J. B.), Catechism of Christian Doctrine. illustrated with passages from the Holy Scriptures. 2s. 6d.

———— Threshold of the Catholic Church. A Course of Plain Instructions for those entering her Communion. 12mo., 4s.

BAGSHAWE (Rt. Rev. Dr.), The Life of our Lord, commemorated in the Mass. 18mo., 6d., bound 1s.; Verses and Hymns separately, 1d., bound 4d.

BAKER (Fr., O.S.B.), The Rule of S. Benedict. From the old English edition of 1638. 12mo., 6d.

Baker's Boy ; or, Life of General Drouot. 18mo., 6d.

BAMPFIELD (Rev. G.), Sir Ælfric and other Tales. 18mo., 6d.; cloth, 1s.: gilt, 1s. 6d.

BARGE (Rev. T.), Occasional Prayers for Festivals. 32mo., 4d. and 6d.; gilt, 1s.

Battista Varani (B.), *see* Veronica (S.). 12mo., 5s.

Battle of Connemara. By Kathleen O'Meara. 12mo.. 3s.

BAUGHAN (Rosa), Shakespeare. Expurgated edition. 8vo., 6s. The Comedies only, 3s. 6d.

Before the Altar. 32mo., 6d.

BELL'S Modern Reader and Speaker. 12mo.. 3s. 6d.

BELLECIO (Fr.), Spiritual Exercises of S. Ignatius. Translated by Dr. Hutch. 18mo., 2s.

BELLINGHAM (Lady Constance) The Duties of Christian Parents. Conferences by Père Matignon. Translated. 12mo.. 5s.

Bells of the Sanctuary,—A Daughter of St. Dominick. By Grace Ramsay. 12mo.. 1s. and 1s. 6d.; stronger bound, 2s.

Benedict (S.), Abridged Explanation of his Medal. 1d.

———— The Rule of our most Holy Father S. Benedict, Patriarch of Monks. From the old English edition of 1638. Edited in Latin and English by one of the Benedictine Fathers of St. Michael's, near Hereford. 12mo., 4s. 6d.

Benedictine Breviary. 4 vols., 18mo., Dessain, 1870. 26s. nett ; morocco, 42s. nett, and 47s. nett.

Benedictine Missal. Pustet, Folio, 1873. 20s. nett; morocco, 50s. nett, and 60s. nett. Dessain, 4to., 1862, 18s. nett ; morocco, 40s. nett, and 50s. nett.

BENNI (Most Rev. C. B.), **Tradition of the Syriac Church of Antioch**, concerning the Primacy and Prerogatives of S. Peter and of his successors, the Roman Pontiffs. 8vo., 7s. 6d.

BENVENUTO BAMBOZZI (Fr., O.M.C.), of the Conventual Friars Minor, Life of, from the Italian (2nd edition) of Fr. Nicholas Treggiari, D.D. 12mo., 5s. *In the Press.*

Berchmans (Bl. John), **New Miracle at Rome**, through the intercession of Bl. John Berchmans. 12mo., 2d.

Bernardine (St.) **of Siena, Life of.** With Portrait. 12mo., 5s.

Bertha ; or, the Consequences of a Fault. 8vo., 2s. 6d.

Bessy ; or, the Fatal Consequence of Telling Lies. 12mo., 1s.; stronger bound, 1s. 6d.; gilt, 2s.

BESTE (J. R. Digby, Esq.), **Catholic Hours.** 32mo., 2s ; red edges, 2s. 6d. ; roan, 3s.; morocco, 6s.

—————— **Church Hymns.** (Latin and English.) 32mo., 6d.

—————— **Holy Readings.** 32mo., 2s., 2s. 6d. ; roan, 3s. ; mor., 6s.

BESTE (Rev. Fr.), **Victories of Rome.** 8vo., 1s.

Bible. Douay Version. 12mo., 3s. ; Persian, 8s. ; morocco, 10s. 6d. 18mo., 2s. 6d. ; Persian, 5s.; calf or morocco, 7s.; gilt, 8s. 6d. 8vo. with borders round pages, Persian calf, 21s., morocco, 25s. 4to., Illustrated, cloth, 21s.; leather extra, 31s. 6d.; Illustrated, morocco, £5 5s. ; superior, £6 6s.

Bible History for the use of Schools. By Gilmour. 12mo., 2s.

—————— By a Teacher. 12mo., 5s.

Blessed Lord. *See* Ribadeneira ; Rutter (Rev. H.).

Blessed Virgin, Devotions to. From Ancient Sources. *See* Regina Sæculorum. 12mo., 1s. and 3s.

—————— **Devout Exercise in honour of.** From the Psalter and Prayers of S. Bonaventure, 32mo., 1s.

—————— **History of.** By Orsini. Translated by Provost Husenbeth. Illustrated, 12mo., 3s. 6d.

—————— **Life of.** In verse. By C. E. Tame, Esq. 16mo., 2s.

—————— **Life of.** Proposed as a model to Christian women. 12mo., 1s.

—————— **in North America, Devotion to.** By Fr. Macleod. 5s.

—————— **Veneration of.** By Mrs. Stuart Laidlaw. 16mo., 4d.

—————— *See* Our Lady, p. 22 ; Leaflets, p. 16 ; May, p. 19.

Blindness, Cure of, through the Intercession of Our Lady and S. Ignatius. 12mo., 2d.

BLOSIUS, Spiritual Works of :—The Rule of the Spiritual Life ; The Spiritual Mirror ; String of Spiritual Jewels. Edited by Rev. Fr. Bowden. 12mo., 3s. 6d.; red edges, 4s.

Blue Scapular, Origin of. 18mo., 1d.

BLYTH (Rev. Fr.), **Devout Paraphrase on the Seven Penitential Psalms.** To which is added "Necessity of Purifying the Soul," by St. Francis de Sales. 18mo., 1s. stronger bound, 1s. 6d.; red edges, 2s.

BONA (Cardinal), **Easy Way to God.** Translated by Father Collins. 12mo., 3s.

BONAVENTURE (S.), **Devout Exercise in honour of Our Lady.** 32mo., 1s.

BONAVENTURE (S.), Life of St. Francis of Assisi. 3s. 6d.
Boniface (S.), Life of. By Mrs. Hope. 12mo., 6s.
BORROMEO (S. Charles), Rules for a Christian Life. 2d.
BOUDON (Mgr.), Book of Perpetual Adoration. Translated by Rev. Dr. Redman. 12mo., 3s.; red edges, 3s. 6d.
BOUDRÉAUX (Rev. J., S.J.), God our Father. 12mo., 4s.
———— Happiness of Heaven. 12mo., 4s.
———— Paradise of God. 12mo., 4s.
BOURKE (Rev. Ulick J.), Easy Lessons : or, Self-Instruction in Irish. 12mo., 2s. 6d.
BOWDEN (Rev. Fr. John), Spiritual Works of Louis of Blois. 12mo., 3s. 6d.; red edges, 4s.
———— Oratorian Lives of the Saints. (Page 22).
BOWDEN (Mrs.), Lives of the First Religious of the Visitation of Holy Mary. 2 vols., 12mo., 10s.
BOWLES (Emily), Eagle and Dove. Translated from the French of Mdlle. Zénaïde Fleuriot. 12mo., 2s. 6d. and 5s.
BRADBURY (Rev. Fr.), Journey of Sophia and Eulalis to the Palace of True Happiness. 12mo., 1s. 6d.; 3s. 6d
BRICKLEY'S Standard Table Book. 32mo., ½d.
BRIDGES (Miss), Sir Thomas Maxwell and his Ward. 12mo., 1s. and 2s.
Bridget (S.), Life of, and other Saints of Ireland. 12mo., 1s.
Brigit (S.) Life of, &c. By M. F. Cusack. 8vo., 6s.
Broken Chain. A Tale. 18mo., 6d.
BROWNE (E. G. K., Esq.), Monastic Legends. 8vo., 6d.
BROWNLOW (Rev. W. R. B.), Church of England and its Defenders. 8vo., 1st letter, 6d.; 2nd letter, 1s.
———— "Vitis Mystica"; or, the True Vine : a Treatise on the Passion of our Lord. 18mo., 4s.; red edges, 4s. 6d.
BUCKLEY (Rev. M.), Sermons, Lectures, &c. 12mo., 6s.
BURDER (Abbot), Confidence in the Mercy of God. By Mgr. Languet. 12mo., 3s.
———— The Consoler; or, Pious Readings addressed to the Sick and all who are afflicted. By Père Lambilotte. 12mo., 4s. 6d.; red ed., 5s.
———— Souls in Purgatory. 32mo., 3d.
———— Novena for the Souls in Purgatory. 32mo., 3d.
Burial of the Dead. For Children and Adults. (Latin and English.) Clear type edition, 32mo., 6d.; roan, 1s. 6d.
Burke (Edmund), Life of. *See* Robertson (Professor).
BURKE (S.H., M.A.), Men and Women of the English Reformation. 12mo., 2 vols., 13s.; Vol. II., 5s.
BURKE (Rev. T. N.), Lectures and Sermons. 2 vols., 24s.
BURKE (Father), and others, Catholic Sermons. 12mo.,2s.
BUTLER (Alban), Lives of the Saints. 2 vols., 8vo., 28s.; gilt, 34s.; 4 vols., 8vo., 32s.; gilt, 50s.; leather, 64s.
———— One Hundred Pious Reflections. 18mo., 1s. and 2s.
BUTLER (Dr.), Catechisms. 1st, ½d.; 2nd, 1d.; 3rd, 1½d.
CALIXTE—Life of the Ven. Anna Maria Taigi. Translated by A. V. Smith Sligo. 8vo., 2s. 6d. and 5s.

Callista. Dramatised by Dr. Husenbeth. 12mo., 2s.
Captain Rougemont ; or, the Miraculous Conversion. 8vo., 2s. 6d.
Cassilda ; or, the Moorish Princess of Toledo. 8vo., 2s. 6d.
Catechisms—The Catechism of Christian Doctrine. Good
    large type on superfine paper. 32mo., 1d., cloth, 2d. ; interleaved, 8d.
———— The Catechism of Christian Doctrine. Illustrated
    with passages from the Holy Scriptures. By the Rev. J. B. Bag-
    shawe. 12mo., 2s. 6d.
———— made Easy. By Rev. H. Gibson. Vol. II, 4s. ; Vol. III., 4s.
———— for First Confession. By Rev. R. G. Davis. 32mo., 1d.
———— Lessons on Christian Doctrine. 18mo., 1½d.
———— General Catechism of the Christian Doctrine.
    By the Right Rev. Bishop Poirier. 18mo., 9d.
———— By Dr. Butler. 32mo., 1st, ½d.; 18mo., 2nd, 1d.; 3rd, 1½d.
———— By Dr. Doyle. 18mo., 1½d.
———— Fleury's Historical. Complete Edition. 18mo., 1½d.
———— Frassinetti's Dogmatic. 12mo., 3s.
———— of the Council. 12mo., 2d.
———— of Perseverance. By Abbé Gaume. 12mo., Vol. I., 7s. 6d.
Catherine Hamilton. By M. F. S. 12mo., 2s. 6d.; gilt, 3s.
Catherine Grown Older. By M. F. S. 12mo., 2s. 6d.; gilt, 3s.
Catholic Hours. *See* Beste (J. R. Digby).
Catholic Keepsake. A Gift Book for all Seasons. 12mo., 6s.
Catholic Piety. *See* Prayer Books, page 30.
Catholic Sick and Benefit Club. *See* Richardson (Rev. R.).
CHALLONER (Bishop), Grounds of Catholic Doctrine
    Large type edition. 18mo., 4d.
———— Memoirs of Missionary Priests. 8vo., 6s.
———— Think Well on't. 18mo., 2d.; cloth, 6d.
CHAMBERS (F.), The Fair Maid of Kent. An Historica
    and Biographical Sketch. 8vo., 6d.
Chances of War. An Irish Tale. By A. Whitelock. 8vo., 5s.
CHARDON (Abbe), Memoirs of a Guardian Angel. 4s.
Chats about the Rosary. *See* Aunt Margaret's Little Neighbours.
CHAUGY (Mother Frances Magdalen de), Lives of the
    First Religious of the Visitation. 2 vols., 12mo., 10s
Child (The). *See* Dupanloup (Mgr.).
Child's Book of the Passion of Our Lord. 32mo., 6d.
Child (The) of Mary's Manual. Second edition, 32mo. 1s.
Children of Mary in the World, Association of. 32mo., 1d.
Choir, Catholic, Manual. By C. B. Lyons. 12mo., 1s.
Christ bearing His Cross. A Steel Engraving from the Picture
    miraculously given to Blessed Colomba, with a short account of her
    Life. 8vo., 6d.; proofs, 1s.
CHRISTIAN BROTHERS' Reading Books.
Christian Doctrine, Lessons on. 18mo., 1½d.
Christian, Duties of a. By Ven. de la Salle. 12mo., 2s
Christian Politeness. By the same Author. 18mo., 1s.
Christian Teacher. By the same Author. 18mo., 1s. 8d.
Christmas Offering. 32mo., 1s. a 100 ; or 7s. 6d. for 1000.
Christmas (The First) for our dear Little Ones. 4to., 5s.

Chronological Sketches. *See* Murray Lane (H.).
Church Defence. *See* Marshall (T. W. M.).
Church History. By Alzog. 8vo., 3 vols. each 20s.
———————— By Darras. 4 vols., 8vo., 48s.
———————— Compendium. By Noethen. 12mo., 8s.
———————— for Schools. By Noethen. 12mo., 5s. 6d.
Church of England and its Defenders. *See* Brownlow (Rev.).
Cistercian Legends of the XIII. Century. *See* Collins (Fr.).
Cistercian Order : its Mission and Spirit. *See* Collins (Fr.).
Civilization and the See of Rome. *See* Montagu (Lord).
Clare (Sister Mary Cherubini) of S. Francis, Life of. Preface by Lady Herbert. With Portrait. 12mo., 3s. 6d.
Cloister Legends ; or, Convents and Monasteries in the Olden Time. 12mo., 4s.
COGERY (A.), Third French Course, with Vocabulary. 12mo., 2s.
COLLINS (Rev. Fr.), Cistercian Legends of the XIII. Century. 12mo., 3s.   [3s. 6d.
———— Cistercian Order : its Mission and Spirit. 12mo.,
———— Easy Way to God. Translated from the Latin of Cardinal Bona. 12mo., 3s.
———— Spiritual Conferences on the Mysteries of Faith and the Interior Life. 12mo., 5s.
COLOMBIERE (Father Claude de la), The Sufferings of Our Lord. Sermons preached in the Chapel Royal, St. James's, in the year 1677. Preface by Fr. Doyotte, S.J. 18mo., 1s. ; stronger bound, 1s. 6d. ; red edges, 2s.
Colombini (B. Giovanni), Life of. By Belcari. Translated from the editions of 1541 and 1832. With Portrait. 12mo., 3s. 6d.
Columba (S.) Life of, &c. By M. F. Cusack. 8vo., 6s.
Columbkille, or Columba (S.), Life and Prophecies of. By St. Adamnan. 12mo., 3s. 6d.
Comedy of Convocation in the English Church. Edited by Archdeacon Chasuble. 8vo., 2s. 6d. *See* page 18.
COMERFORD (Rev. P.), Handbook of the Confraternity of the Sacred Heart. 18mo., 3d.
———— Month of May for all the Faithful ; or, a Practical Life of the Blessed Virgin. 32mo., 1s.
———— Pleadings of the Sacred Heart. 18mo., 1s.; gilt, 2s.; with the Handbook of the Confraternity, 1s. 6d.
Communion, Prayers for, for Children. Preparation, Mass before Communion, Thanksgiving. 32mo. 1d.
Compendious Statement of the Scripture Doctrine regarding the Nature and chief Attributes of the Kingdom of Christ. By C. F. A. 8vo., 1s.
COMPTON (Herbert), Semi-Tropical Trifles. 12mo., boards, 1s.; extra cloth, 2s. 6d.
Conferences. *See* Collins, Lacordaire, Mermillod, Ravignan.
Confession, Auricular. By Rev. Dr. Melia. 18mo., 1s. 6d.
Confession and Holy Communion : Young Catholic's Guide. By Dr. Kenny. 32mo., 4d.; cloth, 6d.; red edges, 9d.; French morocco, 1s. 6d.; calf or morocco, 2s. 6d.

Confidence in God. By Cardinal Manning. 16mo., 1s.

Confidence in the Mercy of God. By Mgr. Languet. Trans·
lated by Abbot Burder. 12mo., 3s.

Confirmation, Instructions for the Sacrament of. A very
complete book. 18mo., 3d.

CONSCIENCE (Hendrick), The Amulet. 12mo., 4s.

———— The Conscript and Blind Rosa. 12mo., 4s.

———— Count Hugo, of Graenhove. 12mo., 4s.

———— The Fisherman's Daughter. 12mo., 4s.

———— Happiness of being Rich. 12mo., 4s.

————— Ludovic and Gertrude. 12mo., 4s.

———— The Village Innkeeper. 12mo., 4s.

———— Young Doctor. 12mo., 4s.

Consoler (The). By Abbot Burder. 12mo., 4s. 6d. and 5s.

Contemplations on the most Holy Sacrament of the
Altar ; or Devout Meditations to serve as Preparations for, and
Thanksgiving after, Communion. Drawn chiefly from the Holy
Scriptures. 18mo., 1s. and 2s.; red edges, 2s. 6d.

Continental Fish Cook. By M. J. N. de Frederic. 18mo., 1s.

Conversion of the Teutonic Race. By Mrs. Hope. 2 vols, 10s.

Convert Martyr ; or, "Callista." By the Rev. Dr. Newman.
Dramatised by Rev. Dr. Husenbeth. 12mo., 2s.

Convocation, Comedy of. By the Author of "The Oxford
Undergraduate of Twenty Years Ago." 8vo. 2s. 6d.

CORTES (John Donoso), Essays on Catholicism, Libe-
ralism, and Socialism. 12mo., 5s.

CRASSET'S Devout Meditations. Translated. 12mo., 8s.

Crests, The Book of Family. Comprising nearly every bearing
and its blazonry, Surnames of Bearers, Dictionary of Mottoes,
British and Foreign Orders of Knighthood, Glossary of Terms,
and upwards of 4,000 Engravings, Illustrative of Peers, Baronets,
and nearly every Family bearing Arms in England, Wales, Scot-
land, Ireland, and the Colonies, &c. 2 vols., 12mo., 24s.

Crucifixion, The. A large picture for School walls, 1s.

CULPEPPER. Family Herbal, 3s. 6d.; coloured plates, 5s. 6d.

CUSACK (M. F.) :—Sister Mary Francis Clare.

Book of the Blessed Ones. 12mo., 4s. 6d.

Devotions for Public and Private Use at the Way
of the Cross. Illustrated. 32mo., 1s.; red edges, 1s. 6d.

Father Mathew, Life of. 12mo., 2s. 6d.   [2s. 6d.

Good Reading for Sundays and Festivals. 12mo.,

Ireland, Patriot's History of. 18mo., 2s.

Jesus and Jerusalem; or, the Way Home. 12mo., 4s. 6d.

Joseph (S.), Life of. 32mo., 1s.

Life of the Most Rev. Dr. Dixon. 12mo. 7s. 6d.

Lives of St. Columba and St. Brigit. 8vo., 6s.

Mary O'Hagan, Abbess, Life of. 8vo., 6s.

Memorare Mass. 32mo., 2d.

Ned Rusheen. 12mo., 5s.

Nun's Advice to her Girls. 12mo., 2s. 6d.

O'Connell ; his Life and Times. 2 vols. 8vo., 18s

Patrick (S.), Life of. 8vo., 6s., gilt, 10s. ; 32mo., 1s.
Illustrated by Doyle (large edition), 4to., 20s.

Patrick's (S.) Manual. 18mo., 3s. 6d.

Pilgrim's Way to Heaven. 12mo., 4s. 6d.

Stations of the Cross, for Public and Private Use.
Illustrated. 16mo., 1s.; red edges, 1s. 6d.

The Liberator ; his Public Speeches and Letters.
2 vols. 8vo., 18s.

The Spouse of Christ. 12mo., vol. 2, 7s. 6d.

Tim O'Halloran's Choice. 12mo., 3s. 6d.

Tronson's Conferences. 12mo., 4s. 6d.

DARRAS (Abbe), History of the Church. 4 vols., 8vo., 48s.

Daughter (A) of S. Dominick : (Bells of the Sanctuary). By
Grace Ramsay. 12mo., 1s. and 1s. 6d. ; better bound, 2s.

DAVIS (F.), Earlier and Later Leaves ; or, an Autumn
Gathering. Poems and Songs. 12mo., 6s.

DAVIS (Rev. R. G.) Catechism for First Confession.' 1d.

———— Garden of the Soul. *See* page 32.

DEAN (Rev. J. Joy), Devotion to Sacred Heart. 12mo., 2s.

DECHAMPS (Mgr.), The Life of Pleasure. 12mo., 1s. 6d.

DE DOSS (P. A., S.J.), The Pearl among the Virtues ; 3s.

Defence of the Roman Church. *See* Gueranger.

DEHAM (Rev. F.) Sacred Heart of Jesus, offered to the
Piety of the Young engaged in Study. 32mo., 6d.

Diary of a Confessor of the Faith. 12mo., 1s.

Directorium Asceticum. By Scaramelli. 4 vols., 12mo., 24s.

DIXON (Fr., O.P.) Albert the Great: his Life and Scho-
lastic Labours. From original documents. By Dr. Sighart.
With Photographic Portrait. 8vo. 10s. 6d. Cheap edition, 5s.

———— Life of St. Vincent Ferrer. From the French of Rev.
Fr. Pradel. With a Photograph. 12mo., 5s.

DOYLE (Canon, O.S.B.), Life of Gregory Lopez, the
Hermit. With a Photographic Portrait. 12mo., 3s. 6d.

DOYLE (Dr.), Catechism. 18mo., 1½d.

DOYOTTE (Rev. Fr., S.J.), Elevations to the Heart of
Jesus. 12mo., 3s.

———— Sufferings of Our Lord. *See* Columbiere (Fr.)

DRAMAS, &c.—Convert Martyr ; or, "Callista" dramatised. 2s.

———— The Duchess Transformed. By W. H. A. (Girls, 1
Act). A Comedy. 12mo., 6d.

——— Ernscliff Hall (Girls, 3 Acts). Drama. 12mo., 6d.

——— Filiola (Girls, 4 Acts). Drama. 12mo., 6d.

——— He would be a Lord (Boys, 3 Acts), a Comedy. 2s.

——— Major John Andre [Historical] (Boys, 5 Acts), 2s.

——— Reverse of the Medal (Girls, 4 Acts). Drama. 6d.

——— Shandy Maguire (Boys, 2 Acts), a Farce. 12mo., 2s.

——— St. Eustace (Boys, 5 Acts). Drama. 12mo., 1s.

——— St. Louis in Chains (Boys, 5 Acts). Drama. 12mo., 2s.

——— St. William of York (Boys, 2 Acts). Drama. 12mo., 6d.

———— Whittington and his Cat. Drama for Children.
9 Scenes. By Henrietta Fairfield. 6d.

———— *See* Shakespeare.

Duchess (The), Transformed. By W. H. A. 12mo., 6d.

DUMESNIL (Abbe), **Recollections of the Reign of Terror.** 12mo., 2s. 6d.

DUPANLOUP (Mgr.), Contemporary Prophecies. 8vo., 1s.

———— **The Child.** Translated by Kate Anderson. 12mo., 3s. 6d.

Dusseldorf Gallery. 357 Engravings. Large 4to. Half-morocco, gilt, £5 5s. nett.

———— 134 Engravings. Large 8vo. Half-morocco, gilt, 42s.

Dusseldorf Society for the Distribution of Good Religious Pictures. Subscription, 8s. 6d. a year. *Catalogue* 3d.

Duties of a Christian. By Ven. de la Salle. 12mo., 2s.

Eagle and Dove. *See* Bowles (Emily).

E. A. M. Countess Adelstan. 12mo., 1s. and 2s. 6d.

———— **Paul Seigneret.** 12mo., 6d., 1s., 1s. 6d., gilt, 2s.

———— **Regina Sæculorum.** 12mo., 1s. and 3s.

———— **Rosalie.** 12mo., 1s., 1s. 6d., gilt, 2s.

Easy Way to God. By Cardinal Bona. 12mo., 3s.

Ebba ; or, the Supernatural Power of the Blessed Sacrament. *This book is in French.* 12mo., 1s. 6d. ; cloth, 2s. 6d.

Electricity and Magnetism ; an Enquiry into the Nature and Results of. By Amyclanus. Illustrated. 12mo., 6s. 6d.

England, History of. *See* Evans.

Epistles and Gospels. Good clear type edition, 32mo., 6d.; roan, 1s. 6d.; larger edition, 18mo., French morocco, 2s.

————, **Explanation of.** By Rev. F. Goffine. Illustrated, 8vo., 9s.

Epistles of S. Paul, Exposition of. *See* MacEvilly (Rt. Rev. Dr.)

Ernscliff Hall. A Drama in Three Acts, for Girls. 12mo., 6d.

Eucharistic Year. 18mo., 4s.

Eucharist (The) and the Christian Life. *See* La Bouillerie.

Europe, Modern, History of. With Preface by Bishop Weathers. 12mo., 5s.; roan, 5s. 6d.; cloth gilt, 6s.

Eustace (St.). A Drama in 5 Acts for Boys. By Rev. T. Meyrick, M.A. 12mo., 1s.

EVANS (L.), History of England, adapted for Junior Classes in Schools. 9d., or separately : Part 1 (Standard 4) 2d. Part 2 (Standard 4) 2d. Part 3 (Standard 5) 3d.

———— **Chronological Outline of English History.** 1½d.

———— **Milton's l'Allegro** (Oxford Local Exam.). 2d.

———— **Parsing and Analysis Table.** 1d.

FAIRFIELD (Henrietta), Whittington and his Cat. A Drama, in 9 Scenes, for Children. 12mo., 6d.

Fairy Ching (The); or, the Chinese Fairies' Visit to England. By Henrica Frederic. 12mo., 1s. ; gilt edges, 1s. 6d.

Fairy Tales for Little Children. By Madeleine Howley Meehan. 12mo., 6d.; stronger bound, 1s. and 1s. 6d.; gilt, 2s.

Faith of Our Fathers. *See* Gibbons (Most Rev. Archbishop).

Fall, Redemption, and Exaltation of Man. 12mo., 1s.

Familiar Instructions on Christian Truths. By a Priest. 12mo., 10d.

FARRELL (Rev. J.), Lectures of a certain Professor. 7s. 6d.

FAVRE (Abbe), Heaven Opened by the Practice of Frequent Confession and Communion. 12mo., 2s. ; stronger bound, 3s. 6d.; red edges, 4s.

Feasts (The) of Camelot, with the Tales that were told there. By Mrs. T. K. Hervey. 12mo., 3s. 6d., or in 2 vols. 1s. each.

FERRIS (Rev. D.), Life of St. Mary Frances of the Five Wounds of Jesus Christ. From the Italian. 12mo., 3s. 6d.

Filiola. A Drama in Four Acts, for Girls. 12mo., 6d.

First Apostles of Europe. *See* Hope (Mrs.).

First Communion and Confirmation Memorial. Beautifully printed in gold and colours, folio, 1s. each, or 9s. a dozen, nett.

First Religious of the Visitation of Holy Mary, Lives of. With two Photographs. 2 vols., 12mo., 10s.

FLEET (Charles), Tales and Sketches. 8vo., 2s.; stronger bound, 2s. 6d.; gilt, 3s. 6d.

FLEURIOT (Mlle. Zenaide), Eagle and Dove. Translated by Emily Bowles. 12mo., 2s. 6d. and 5s.

FLEURY'S Historical Catechism. Large edition, 12mo., 1½d.

Flowers of Christian Wisdom. *See* Henry (Lucien).

Fluffy. A Tale for Boys. By M. F. S. 12mo., 3s. 6d.

Following of Christ. *See* A'Kempis.

Foreign Books. *See* R. W.'s Catalogue of Foreign Books. 3d.

Francis of Assisi (S.) Life of. By S. Bonaventure. Translated by Miss Lockhart. 12mo., 3s. 6d.

FRANCIS OF SALES (S.), Consoling Thoughts. 18mo., 2s.

———— The Mystical Flora ; or, the Christian Life under the Emblem of Saints. 4to., 8s.

———— Necessity of Purifying the Soul. *See* Blyth (Rev. Fr.).

———— Sweetness of Holy Living. 18mo., 1s.; levant, 3s.

Franciscan Annals and Monthly Bulletin of the Third Order of St. Francis. 8vo., 6d.

FRANCO (Rev. S.) Devotions to the Sacred Heart. 12mo., 4s.; cheap edition, 2s.

FRASSINETTI—Dogmatic Catechism. 12mo., 3s.

FREDERIC (Henrica), The Fairy Ching ; or, the Chinese Fairies' Visit to England. 12mo., 1s.; gilt edges, 1s. 6d.

FREDERIC (M. J. N. de), Continental Fish Cook ; or, a Few Hints on Maigre Dinners. 18mo., 1s., soiled covers, 6d.

Freemasons, Irish and English, and their Foreign Brothers. 4to., 2s.

From Sunrise to Sunset. By L. B. 12mo., 3s. 6d.

GALLERY (Rev. D.), Handbook of Essentials in History and Literature, Ancient and Modern. 18mo., 1s.

Garden of the Soul. *See* page 32.

Garden (Little) of the Soul. *See* page 30.

Gathered Gems from Spanish Authors. *See* Monteiro.

GAUME (Abbe), Catechism of Perseverance. 4 vols., 12mo. Vol. 1, 7s. 6d.

GAYRARD (Mme. Paul) Harmony of the Passion. Compiled from the four Gospels, in Latin and French. 18mo., 1s. 6d.

German (S.), Life of. 12mo., 3s. 6d.

GIBBONS (Most Rev. Archbishop), The Faith of Our Fathers; Being a Plain Exposition and Vindication of the Church Founded by our Lord Jesus Christ. 12mo., 4s. Paper covers, 2s.

GIBSON (Rev. H.), Catechism made Easy. 12mo., Vol. I. (out of print); Vol. II., 4s. ; Vol. III., 4s.

GILMOUR (Rev. R.), Bible History for the Use of Schools. Illustrated. 12mo., 2s.

God our Father. By a Father of the Society of Jesus. 12mo., 4s.

GOFFINE (Rev. F.), Explanation of the Epistles and Gospels. Illustrated. 8vo., 9s.

Good Thoughts for Priests and People. *See* Noethen.

Gospels, An Exposition of. *See* MacEvilly (Most Rev. Dr.).

Grace before and after Meals. 32mo., 1d. ; cloth, 2d.

GRACE RAMSAY. A Daughter of S. Dominick (Bells of the Sanctuary, No. 4). 12mo., 1s. ; stronger bound, 1s. 6d. and 2s.

———— *See* O'Meara (Kathleen).

GRACIAN (Fr. Baltasar), Sanctuary Meditations for Priests and Frequent Communicants. Translated from the Spanish by Mariana Monteiro. 12mo., 4s.

Grains of Gold. Counsels for the Sanctification and Happiness of Life. 18mo., 1st Series, 6d.; cloth, 1s. 16mo., Series 1 and 2, cloth, 2s. 6d.

GRANT (Bishop), Pastoral on St. Joseph. 32mo., 4d. & 6d.

Gregorian, or Plain Chant and Modern Music. 8vo., 2s. 6d.

Gregory Lopez, the Hermit, Life of. By Canon Doyle, O.S.B. With a Photographic Portrait. 12mo., 3s. 6d.

Grounds of the Catholic Doctrine. By Bishop Challoner. Large type edition, 18mo., 4d.

Guardian Angel, Memoirs of a. By Abbé Chardon. 12mo., 4s.

GUERANGER (Dom), Defence of the Roman Church against F. Gratry. Translated by Canon Woods. 8vo., 1s.

Guide to Sacred Eloquence. *See* Passionist Fathers.

HALL (E.), Munster Firesides. 12mo., 3s. 6d.

Happiness of Being Rich. By Conscience. 12mo., 4s.

Happiness of Heaven. By a Father of the Society of Jesus. 12mo. 4s.

Harmony of Anglicanism. By T. W. Marshall. 8vo., 2s. 6d.

HAY (Bishop), Sincere Christian. 18mo., 2s. 6d.

———— **Devout Christian.** 18mo., 2s. 6d.

He would be a Lord. A Comedy in 3 Acts. (Boys). 12mo., 2s.

Heaven Opened by the Practice of frequent Confession and Holy Communion. By the Abbé Favre. 12mo., 2s. ; stronger bound, 3s. 6d.; red edges, 4s.

HEDLEY (Bishop), Five Sermons—Light of the Holy Spirit in the World. 12mo., 1s.; cloth, 1s. 6d. Revelation, Mystery, Dogma and Creeds, Infallibility : separately, 3d. each.

HEIGHAM (John), A Devout Exposition of the Holy Mass. Edited by Austin John Rowley, Priest. 12mo., 4s.

Henri V. (Comte de Chambord). *See* Walsh (W. H.).

HENRY (Lucien), Flowers of Christian Wisdom. 18mo., 1s. and 2s.; red edges, 2s. 6d.

Herbal, Brook's Family. 12mo., 3s. 6d.; coloured plates, 5s. 6d.

HERBERT (Wallace), My Dream and Verses Miscellaneous. With a frontispiece. 12mo., 5s.

———— **The Angels and the Sacraments.** 16mo., 1s.

HERGENRÖTHER (Dr.), Anti-Janus. Translated by Professor Robertson. 12mo., 6s.

HERVEY (Eleanora Louisa),‾ My Godmother's Stories from many Lands. 12mo., 3s. 6d.

———— **Our Legends and Lives.** 12mo., 6s.

———— **Rest, on the Cross.** 12mo., 3s. 6d.

———— **The Feasts of Camelot, with the Tales that were told there.** 12mo., 3s. 6d. ; or, separately: Christmas 1s. ; Whitsuntide, 1s.

HILL (Rev. Fr.), Elements of Philosophy, comprising Logic and General Principles of Metaphysics. 8vo., 6s.

HOFFMAN (Franz), Industry and Laziness. 12mo., 3s.

Holy Childhood. A book of simple Prayers and Instructions for very little children. 32mo., 6d. or 1s. ; gilt, 1s. 6d.

Holy Church the Centre of Unity. *See* Shaw (T. H.)

Holy Communion. By Hubert Lebon. 12mo., 4s.

Holy Family, Confraternity of. *See* Manning (Card.).

Holy Places : their Sanctity and Authenticity. *See* Philpin.

Holy Readings. *See* Beste (J. R. Digby Esq.).

HOPE (Mrs.), The First Apostles of Europe ; or, "The Conversion of the Teutonic Race." 2 vols., 12mo., 10s.

Horace. Literally translated by Smart. 18mo., 2s.

HUGUET (Pere), The Power of S. Joseph. Meditations and Devotions. Translated by Clara Mulholland. 1s. 6d.

HUMPHREY (Rev. W., S.J.), The Panegyrics of Fr. Segneri, S.J. Translated from the orignal Italian. With a Preface by the Rev. W. Humphrey, S.J. 12mo., 5s.

HUSENBETH (Rev. Dr.), Convert Martyr. 12mo., 2s.

———— **History of the Blessed Virgin.** Translated from Orsini. Illustrated. 12mo., 3s. 6d. [Illustrated. 12mo., 5s.

———— **Life and Sufferings of Our Lord.** By Rev. H. Rutter.

———— **Life of Mgr. Weedall.** 8vo., 1s.

———— **Little Office of the Immaculate Conception.** In Latin and English. 32mo., 4d. ; cloth, 6d.; roan, 1s. ; calf or morocco, 2s. 6d.

———— **Our Blessed Lady of Lourdes.** 18mo., 6d.; with the Novena, 1s.; cloth, 1s. 6d. Novena, separately, 4d.; Litany, 1d.

———— **Roman Question.** 8vo., 6d.

Husenbeth (Provost), Sermon on his Death. By Very Rev. Canon Dalton. 8vo. 6d.

HUTCH (Rev. W., D.D.), Nano Nangle, her Life and her Labours. 12mo., 7s. 6d.

Hymn Book. Complete, for Missions. 32mo., 1d.; cloth, 2d.

Hymn Book (The Catholic). Edited by Rev. G. L. Vere. 32mo., 2d.; cloth, 4d.; Appendix (Hymns to Saints), 1d.

Iceland (Three Sketches of Life in). By Carl Andersen. 12mo.

IGNATIUS (S.), Spiritual Exercises. By Fr. Bellecio, S.J. Translated by Dr. Hutch. 18mo., 2s.

Ignatius (S.), Cure of Blindness through the Intercession of Our Lady and S. Ignatius. 12mo., 2d.

Illustrated Manual of Prayers. 32mo., 3d.; cloth, 4d.
Imitation of Christ. *See* A'Kempis.
Immaculate Conception, Definition of. 12mo., 6d.
———— Little Office of. *See* Husenbeth (Rev. Dr.).
———— Little Office of, in Latin and English. 32mo., 1d.
Indulgences. *See* Maurel (Rev. F. A.).
Industry and Laziness. By Franz Hoffman. From the German by James King. 12mo., 3s.
Infallibility of the Pope. By the Author of "The Oxford Undergraduate of Twenty Years Ago." 8vo., 1s.
In Suffragiis Sanctorum. Commem. S. Josephi ; Commem. S. Georgii. Set of 5 for 4d.
Insula Sanctorum : The Island of Saints. 12mo., 1s.
Insurrection of '98. By Rev. P. F. Kavanagh. 12mo., 2s. 6d.
IOTA. The Adventures of a Protestant in Search of a Religion : being the Story of a late Student of Divinity at Bunyan Baptist College ; a Nonconformist Minister, who seceded to the Catholic Church. 12mo., 3s. 6d. ; cheap edition, 2s.
Ireland (History of). By Miss Cusack. 18mo., 2s. A large edition, illustrated by Doyle, 8vo., 11s.
Ireland (History of). By T. Young. 18mo., 2s. 6d.
Ireland Ninety Years ago. 12mo., 1s.
Ireland, Popular Poetry of. (Songs). 262 pages, 18mo., 6d.
Ireland, Revelations of, in the Past Generation. 12mo., 1s.
Irish Board Reading Books.
Irish First Book. 18mo., 2d. Second Book. 18mo., 4d.
Irish Monthly. 8vo. Vol. 1877, cloth, 8s.
Italian Revolution (The History of). The History of the Barricades. By Keyes O'Clery, M.P. 8vo., 7s. 6d. and 3s. 6d.
JACOB (W. J.), Personal Recollections of Rome. 6d.
JENKINS (Rev. O. L.) Student's Handbook of British and American Literature. 12mo., 8s.
Jesuits (The), and other Essays. *See* Nevin (Willis, Esq.)
Jesus and Jerusalem ; or, the Way Home. *See* Cusack (Miss).
John of God (S.), Life of. With Photographic Portrait. 12mo., 5s.
Joseph (S.), Life of. By Miss Cusack. 32mo., 6d.; cloth, 1s.
———— Novena of Meditations. 18mo., 1s.
———— Novena to, with a Pastoral by the late Bishop Grant. 32mo., 4d.; cloth, 6d.
———— Power of. *See* Huguet.
———— *See* Leaflets.
Journey of Sophia and Eulalie to the Palace of True Happiness. From the French by Rev. Fr. Bradbury. 12mo., 1s. 6d.; better bound, 3s. 6d.
KAVANAGH (Rev. P. F.), Insurrection of '98. 1s. 6d.
Keighley Hall, and other Tales. By E. King. 18mo., 6d.; cloth, 1s. ; stronger bound, 1s. 6d. ; gilt, 2s.
KEMEN (Charles), The Marpingen Apparitions. 8vo., 1s.
KENNY (Dr.), Young Catholic's Guide to Confession and Holy Communion. 32mo., 4d.; cloth, 6d.; red edges, 9d.; roan, 1s. 6d.; calf or morocco, 2s. 6d.

R. Washbourne, 18 *Paternoster Row, London.*

KENNY (Dr.), **New Year's Gift to our Heavenly Father.**
32mo., 4d.

KERNEY (M. T.), **Compendium of History.** 12mo., 5s.

Key of Heaven. *See* Prayers, page 31.

KINANE (Rev. T. H.), **Dove of the Tabernacle.** 1s. 6d.

———— **Angel (The) of the Altar;** or, the Love of the Most
Adorable and Most Sacred Heart of Jesus. 18mo., 2s. 3d.

———— **Mary Immaculate, Mother of God;** or Devotions in
honour of the B.V.M. 18mo., 2s.

KING (Elizabeth), **Keighley Hall, and other Tales.**
18mo., 6d.; cloth, 1s.; stronger bound, 1s. 6d.; gilt, 2s.

———— **The Silver Teapot.** 18mo., 4d.

KING (James). Industry and Laziness. 12mo., 3s.

Kishoge Papers. Tales of Devilry and Drollery. 12mo., 1s. 6d.

LA BOUILLERIE (Mgr. de), **The Eucharist and the
Christian Life.** Translated by L. C. 12mo., 3s. 6d.

LACORDAIRE'S Conferences. 12mo., On Life, 3s. 6d.;
God, 6s.; Jesus Christ, 6s.

Lacordaire. The Inner Life of Pere Lacordaire. From
the French of Père Chocarne. 12mo., 6s. 6d.

Lady Mildred's Housekeeper, A Few Words from. 2d.

LAIDLAW (Mrs. Stuart), **Letters to my God-child.**
No. 4. On the Veneration of the Blessed Virgin. 16mo., 4d.

LAING (Rev. Dr.), **Blessed Virgin's Root traced in the
Tribe of Ephraim.** 8vo., 10s. 6d.

———— **Descriptive Guide to the Mass.** 12mo., 1s. and 1s. 6d.

———— **Knight of the Faith.** 12mo., 4s.

Absurd Protestant Opinions concerning *Intention.* 4d.

Catholic, not Roman Catholic. 4d.

Challenge to the Churches. 1d.

Favourite Fallacy about Private Judgment and Inquiry. 1d.

Protestantism against the Natural Moral Law. 1d.

What is Christianity? 6d.

Whence does the Monarch get his right to Rule? 2s. 6d.

LAMBILOTTE (Pere), **The Consoler.** Translated by Abbot
Burder. 12mo., 4s. 6d.; red edges, 5s.

LANGUET (Mgr.), **Confidence in the Mercy of God.**
Translated by Abbot Burder. 12mo., 3s.

Last of the Catholic O'Malleys. By M. Taunton. 18mo.,
1s. 6d.; stronger bound, 2s.

Leaflets. 1d. each, or 1s. 2d. per 100 post free.

Act of Reparation to the Sacred Heart.

Archconfraternity of the Agonising Heart of Jesus and the
Compassionate Heart of Mary : Prayers for the Dying.

Archconfraternity of Our Lady of Angels.

Ditto, Rules.

Christmas Offering (or 7s. 6d. a 1000).

Devotions to S. Joseph.

Gospel according to St. John, *in Latin.* 1s. 6d. per 100.

Indulgenced Prayers for Souls in Purgatory.

Indulgences attached to Medals, Crosses, Statues, &c., by the Blessing of His Holiness and of those privileged to give his Blessing.

Intentions for Indulgences.

Litany of Our Lady of Angels.

Litany of S. Joseph, and Devotions.

Litany of Resignation.

Miraculous Prayer—August Queen of Angels.

Picture of Crucifixion, " I thirst " (or 5s. a 1000).

Prayer for One's Confessor.

Union of our Life with the Passion of our Lord.

Visit to the Blessed Sacrament.   5s. per 100.

Leaflets.   1d. each, or 6s. per 100.

Act of Consecration to the Sacred Heart.

Concise Portrait of the Blessed Virgin.

Explanation of the Medal or Cross of St. Benedict.

Indulgenced Prayers for the Rosary of the Dead.

Indulgenced Prayer before a Crucifix.

Litany of the Seven Dolours.

Prayer to S. Philip Neri.

Prayers before and after Holy Communion.

Revelation made by the mouth of Our Saviour to St. Bridget.

LEBON (Hubert), Holy Communion. 12mo., 4s.

Legends of the Saints.   By M. F. S.   16mo., 3s. 6d.

Lenten Thoughts. By Bishop Amherst. 18mo., 2s.; red edges, 2s. 6d.

LEO XIII., The Church and Civilisation.   8vo., 2s.

Letter to George Augustus Simcox.   8vo., 6d.

Letters to My God-child. By Mrs. Stuart Laidlaw.   16mo., 4d.

Life in the Cloister. By Miss Stewart. 12mo., 3s. 6d.

Life of Pleasure.   By Mgr. Dechamps. 12mo., 1s. 6d.

Light of the Holy Spirit in the World.   Five Sermons, by Bishop Hedley.   12mo., 1s.; cloth, 1s. 6d.

LIGUORI (S.), Fourteen Stations of the Cross.   18mo., 1d.

——— **Selva ;** or, a Collection of Matter for Sermons.   12mo., 5s.

——— **Way of Salvation.**   32mo., 1s.

——— **Life of.**   12mo., 10s.

——— **Officium Parvum.**   Latin and English.   With Novena. 12mo., 1s.; cloth, 2s.; red edges, 3s.

Lily of S. Joseph : A little manual of Prayers and Hymns for Mass.   64mo., 2d.; cloth, 3d., 4d., and 6d.; gilt, 8d.; roan, 1s.; French morocco, 1s. 6d.; calf or morocco, 2s.; gilt, 2s. 6d.

Literature, Philosophy of, An Essay contributing to a. By B. A. M.   12mo., 6s.

Literature, Student's Handbook.   *See* Jenkins (Rev. O. L.).

Little Prayer Book.   32mo., 3d.

Lives of the First Religious of the Visitation of Holy Mary.   By Mother Frances Magdalen de Chaugy.   With 2 Photographs.   2 vols., 12mo., 10s.

Lost Children of Mount St. Bernard.   18mo., 6d.

Louis (St.), in Chains.   Drama, Five Acts (Boys).   12mo., 2s.

Lourdes, Our Blessed Lady of. By Rev. Dr. Husenbeth. 18mo., 6d.; with the Novena, 1s.; cloth, 1s. 6d.
———— Novena of, for the use of the Sick. 4d.
———— Litany of. 1d. each.
———— Photograph, Carte de Visite, 1s.; Cabinet, 2s.; 4to., 4s.
Ludovic and Gertrude. By Conscience. 12mo., 4s.
LUCK (Dom Edmund J.), Short Meditations for every Day in the Year. From the Italian. 12mo. Edition for the Regular Clergy, 2 vols., 9s. ; edition for the Secular Clergy and others, 2 vols., 9s.
LYONS (C. B.), Catholic Choir Manual. 12mo., 1s.
———— Catholic Psalmist. 12mo., 4s.   [18mo., 2s.
MACDANIEL (M. A.), Month of May for Interior Souls.
———— Novena to S. Joseph. 32mo., 4d.; cloth, 6d.
———— Road to Heaven. A Game. 3s. 6d.
MACEVILLY (Bishop), Exposition of the Epistles of St. Paul and of the Catholic Epistles. 2 vols., large 8vo. 18s.
———— Exposition of the Gospels. Large 8vo., Vol. I., 12s. 6d.
MACLEOD (Rev. X. D.), Devotion to Our Lady in North America. 8vo., 5s.
Major John Andre. An Historical Drama for Boys. Five Acts. 2s.
MANNING (Cardinal), Church, Spirit and the Word. 6d.
———— Confidence in God. 16mo., 1s.
———— Confraternity of the Holy Family. 8vo., 3d.
———— Glory of S. Vincent de Paul. 12mo., 1s.
———— Independence of the Holy See. 12mo., 5s.
———— True Story of the Vatican Council. 12mo., 5s.
MANNOCK (Patrick), Origin and Progress of Religious Orders, and Happiness of a Religious State. Translated from the Latin of Rev. F. Plætus. 12mo., 2s. 6d.
Manual of Catholic Devotions. *See* Prayers, page 31.
Manual of Devotions in honour of Our Lady of Sorrows. Compiled by the Clergy at St. Patrick's, Soho. 18mo., 1s. & 1s. 6d.
Manual of the Cross and Passion. *See* Passionist Fathers.
Manual of the Sisters of Charity. 18mo., 6s.
Margarethe Verflassen. Translated from the German by Mrs. Smith Sligo. 12mo., 1s. 6d. and 3s.; gilt, 3s. 6d.
Margaret Roper. By A. M. Stewart. 12mo., 6s.; extra, 7s.
Marpingen Apparitions. By C. Kemen. 8vo., 1s.
MARQUIGNY (Pere), Life and Letters of Countess Adelstan. 12mo., 1s. and 2s. 6d.
MARSHALL (A. J. P., Esq.), Comedy of Convocation in the English Church. 8vo., 2s. 6d. *
———— English Religion. 8vo. 6d.,
———— Infallibility of the Pope. 8vo., 1s. *
———— Oxford Undergraduate of Twenty Years Ago. 8vo., 2s. 6d.; cloth, 3s. 6d. *
———— Reply to the Bishop of Ripon's Attack on the Catholic Church. 8vo., 6d. *
MARSHALL (T. W. M., Esq.), Harmony of Anglicanism—Church Defence. 8vo., 2s. 6d. *
          The 5 (*) in one Volume, 8vo., 6s.

MARSHALL (Rev. W.), The Doctrine of Purgatory. 1s.

MARTIN (Rev. E. R.), Rule of the Pope-King. 8vo., 6d.

Mary, A Remembrance of. 32mo., 2s.

Mary Christina of Savoy (Venerable). 18mo., 6d.

Mary Immaculate, Devotion to. By Rev. T. H. Kinane. 2s.

Mass, Descriptive Guide to. By Rev. Dr. Laing. 12mo., 1s., or stronger bound, 1s. 6d.

Mass, Devotions for. Very *Large type*, 18mo., 2d.

Mass (The). *See* Müller (Rev. M.), Tronson (Abbe).

Mass, A Devout Exposition of. *See* Rowley (Rev. A. J.).

Mathew (Father), Life of. By Miss Cusack. 12mo., 2s. 6d.

Matignon (Pere) The Duties of Christian Parents. 12mo. 5s.

MAUREL (Rev. F. A.), Christian Instructed in the Nature and Use of Indulgences. 18mo., 2s.

Maxims of the Kingdom of Heaven. 12mo., 5s.; red edges, 5s. 6d.; calf or mor., 10s. 6d. Old Testament, 1s. 6d.; Gospels, 1s.

May, Month of. By Rev. P. Comerford. 32mo., 1s.

May, Month of. By M. A. Macdaniel. 18mo., 2s.

May, Month of, principally for the use of Religious Communities. 18mo., 1s. 6d.

May Readings for the Feasts of Our Lady. By Rev. A. P. Bethell. 18mo., 1s. 6d.

M'CORRY (Rev. Dr.), Monks of Iona and the Duke of Argyll. 8vo., 3s. 6d.

———— **Rome, Past, Present, Future.** 8vo., 6d.

MEEHAN (M. H.), Fairy Tales for Little Children. 12mo., 6d. and 1s.; stronger bound, 1s. 6d.; gilt, 2s.

MELIA (Rev. Dr.), Auricular Confession. 18mo., 1s. 6d.

MERMILLOD (Mgr.), The Supernatural Life. Translated from the French, with a Preface by Lady Herbert. 12mo., 5s.

MEYRICK (Rev. T.), Life of St. Wenefred. 12mo., 2s.

———— **St. Eustace.** A Drama (5 Acts) for Boys. 12mo., 1s.

M. F. S., Catherine Hamilton. 12mo., 2s. 6d.; gilt, 3s.

———— **Catherine Grown Older.** 12mo., 2s. 6d.; gilt, 3s.

———— **Fluffy.** A Tale for Boys. 12mo., 3s. 6d.

———— **Legends of the Saints.** 16mo., 3s. 6d. [gilt, 1s. 6d.

———— **My Golden Days.** 12mo., 2s. 6d.; or in 3 vols., 1s. ea.

———— **Stories of Holy Lives.** 12mo., 3s. 6d.

———— **Stories of Martyr Priests.** 12mo., 3s. 6d.

———— **Stories of the Saints.** 12mo., 3s. 6d.; gilt, 4s. 6d.

———————— Second Series. 12mo., 3s. 6d.; gilt, 4s. 6d.

———————— Third Series. 12mo., 3s. 6d.

———— **Story of the Life of S. Paul.** 12mo., 2s. 6d.

———— **The Three Wishes.** A Tale. 12mo., 2s. 6d.

———— **Tom's Crucifix,** and other Tales. 12mo., 3s., or in 5 vols., 1s. each, gilt 1s. 6d.

Message from the Mother Heart of Mary. 18mo., 4d. and 6d.

MILES (G. H.), Truce of God. A Tale. 12mo., 4s.

MILNER (Bishop), Devotion to the Sacred Heart of Jesus. 32mo., 3d.; cloth, 6d.; gilt, 1s.

Miracles. A New Miracle at Rome, through the intercession of B. John Berchmans. 12mo., 2d.

———— Cure of Blindness, through the intercession of Our Lady and S. Ignatius. 12mo., 2d.

Mirror of Faith—your Likeness in It. By Fr. Hooker. 3s.

Misgivings—Convictions. 12mo., 6d.

Missal. *See* Prayers, page 31.

Monastic Legends. By E. G. K. Browne. 8vo., 6d.

MOHR (Rev. J., S.J.), Cantiones Sacrae. Hymns and Chants. Music and Words. 8vo., 5s.

———— Manual of Sacred Chant. Music and Words. 18mo. 2s. 6d.

MONK (Rev. Fr., O.S.B.), Daily Exercises. 18mo., 3s. 6d.

Monk of the Monastery of Yuste. *See* Monteiro (Mariana).

Monks of Iona and the Duke of Argyll. *See* M'Corry.

MONSABRE (Rev. Pere), Gold and Alloy. 12mo., 2s. 6d.

MONTAGU (Lord Robert), Civilization and the See of Rome. 8vo., 6d.

Montalembert (Count de). By George White. 12mo., 6d.

MONTEIRO (Mariana), Allah Akbar—God is Great. An Arab Legend of the Siege and Conquest of Granada. 12mo., 3s. 6d.

———— Monk of the Monastery of Yuste ; or, The Last Days of theEmperor Charles V. An Historical Legend of the 16th Century. 12mo., 2s. 6d.

———— Gathered Gems from Spanish Authors. 12mo., 3s.

———— Sanctuary Meditations. *See* Gracian.

MORA (Ven. Elizabeth Canori), Life of. Translated from the Italian, with Preface by Lady Herbert. With Photograph, 12mo. 3s. 6d.

MULHOLLAND (Rosa), Prince and Saviour : The Story of Jesus. 12mo., Coloured Illustrations, 2s. 6d.; 32mo., 6d.

MULLER (Rev. M.), The Holy Mass. 12mo., 10s. 6d.

Multiplication Table, on a sheet. 3s. per 100.

MURRAY-LANE (Chevalier H.), Chronological Sketch of the Kings of England and the Kings of France. 12mo. 2s. 6d.; or in 2 vols., 1s. 6d. each.

MUSIC : Ave Maria, for Four Voices. By W. Schulthes. 1s. 3d.

Cæcilian Society. *See* Separate List. Price 1s. or 2s.

Catholic Hymnal (English Words). For one, two, or four voices, with accompaniment. By Leopold de Prins. 4to., 2s.; bound, 3s.

Cor Jesu, Salus in Te sperantium. By W. Schulthes, 2s.; with Harp Accompaniment, 2s. 6d.; abridged, 3d.

Corona Lauretana. 20 Litanies by W. Schulthes. 2s.

Evening Hymn at the Oratory. By Rev. J. Nary. 3d.

Litanies (36) and Benediction Service. By W. Schulthes. 6s. Second Series (Corona Lauretana). 2s.

Litanies (6). By E. Leslie. 6d.

Litanies (18). By Rev. J. McCarthy. 1s. 3d.

Litany of the B.V.M. By Baronnesse Emma Freemantle. 6d.

Mass of the Holy Child Jesus. In Unison. By

W. Schulthes. 3s. The vocal part only, 4d. ; or 3s. per doz. Cloth, 6d. ; or 4s. 6d. per doz. [Schaller. 2s. 6d.

Mass of St. Patrick. For three equal voices. By F.

Ne projicias me a facie Tua. Motett for Four Voices. By W. Schulthes. 1s. 3d.

Oratory Hymns. By W. Schulthes. 2 vols., 8s.

Recordare. Oratorio Jeremiæ Prophetæ. By the same. 1s.

Regina Cœli. Motett for Four Voices. By W. Schulthes. 3s. Vocal Arrangement, 1s.

Six Sacred Vocal Pieces, for three or four equal Voices. By W. Schulthes. 4s.

Six Invocations, for four equal Voices. By W. Schulthes. 1s. 6d.

Twelve Latin Hymns. By W. Schulthes. 1s. 6d.

Veni Domine. Motett for Four Voices. By W. Schulthes. 2s. Vocal Arrangement, 6d.

Vespers and Benediction Service. Composed and harmonized by Leopold de Prins. 4to., 3s. 6d.

* *All the above (music) prices are nett.*

My Conversion and Vocation. By Rev. Father Schouvaloff, 5s.

My Godmother's Stories from many Lands. By Mrs. T. K. Hervey. 12mo., 3s. 6d.

My Golden Days. By M. F. S. 12mo., 2s. 6d., or in 3 vols., 1s. each ; or 1s. 6d. gilt.

NARY (Rev. J.) Evening Hymn at the Oratory. Music, 3d.

Necessity of Enquiry as to Religion. *See* Pye (Henry John).

NEVIN (Willis, Esq.), The Jesuits, and other Essays. 12mo., 1s. ; cloth, 2s. 6d.

**NEWMAN (Rev. Dr.), Miscellanies, 6s.; Critical and Historical Essays, 2 vols., 12s. ; Tracts, Theological and Ecclesiastical, 8s. ; Certain Difficulties felt by Anglicans, second series, 5s. 6d. Via Media, 2 vols., 12s. Development, 6s.

——— Characteristics from the Writings of.** By W. S. Lilly. 12mo., 6s.

New Testament. 12mo., 2s. 6d. Persian calf, 7s. 6d., morocco, 10s. Illustrated, large 4to., 7s. 6d.

New Year's Gift to Our Heavenly Father. 32mo., 4d.

Nicholas ; or, the Reward of a Good Action. 18mo., 6d.

NICHOLS (T. L.), Forty Years of American Life. 5s.

Nina and Pippo, the Lost Children of Mt. St. Bernard. 6d.

NOETHEN'S (Rev. T.), Good Thoughts for Priests and People ; or, Short Meditations for every Day in the Year. 8s.

——— **Compendium of the History of the Catholic Church.** 12mo., 8s.

——— **History of the Catholic Church.** 12mo., 5s. 6d.

Novena to Our Blessed Lady of Lourdes for the use of the Sick. 18mo., 4d.

Novena of Grace, revealed by S. Francis Xavier. 18mo., 6d.

Novena of Meditations in honour of St. Joseph, according to the method of St. Ignatius, preceded by a new method of hearing Mass according to the intentions of the Souls in Purgatory. 18mo., 1s.

R. Washbourne, 18 *Paternoster Row, London.*

Occasional Prayers for Festivals. *See* Prayers, page 31.

O'CLERY (Keyes, M.P., K.S.G.), The History of the Italian Revolution. First Period—The Revolution of the Barricades (1796-1849). 8vo., 7s. 6d. Cheap edition 3s. 6d.

O'Connell the Liberator. *See* Cusack (M. F.).

O'GALLAGHER (Dr.), Sermons in Irish-Gælic ; with literal idiomatic English Translation, and a Memoir of the Bishop, by Canon U. J. Bourke. 8vo., 7s. 6d.

O'Hagan (Mary), Life of. By Miss Cusack. 8vo., 6s.

O'HAIRE (Rev. J.), Recollections of South Africa. 7s. 6d.

O'MAHONY (D.P.M.), Rome semper eadem. 8vo., 1s. 6d.

O'MEARA (Kathleen), The Battle of Connemara. 12mo., 3s.

———— *See* Grace Ramsay.

On what Authority do I accept Christianity ? 12mo., 6d.

Oratorian Lives of the Saints. With Portrait, 12mo., 5s. a vol.

 I. S. Bernardine of Siena, Minor Observatine.

 II. S. Philip Benizi, Fifth General of the Servites.

 III. S. Veronica Giuliani, and B. Battista Varani.

 IV. S. John of God. By Canon Cianfogni.

O'REILLY (Rev. Dr.), Victims of the Mamertine. 5s.

—————A Romance of Repentance. 12mo., 3s. 6d.

Oremus, A Liturgical Prayer Book. *See* p. 31.

Our Lady's Comfort to the Sorrowful. 32mo., 6d. and 1s.

Our Lady (Devotion to) in North America. *See* Macleod.

Our Lady's Lament. *See* Tame (C.E.).

Our Lady's Month. By Rev. A. P. Bethell. 18mo., 1s. 6d.

Our Legends and Lives. By E. L. Hervey. 12mo., 6s.

Our Lord's Life, Passion, Death, and Resurrection. Translated from Ribadeneira. 12mo., 1s.

———— By Rev. H. Rutter. Illustrated. 12mo., 5s.

———— Incidents. A Series of 12 Illuminations. 4to., 6s.

OXENHAM (H. N.), Dr. Pusey's Eirenicon. 8vo., 6d.

———— Poems. 12mo., 3s. 6d.

Oxford Undergraduate of Twenty Years Ago. By a Bachelor of Arts. 8vo., 2s. 6d.; cloth, 3s. 6d.

OZANAM (A. F.), Protestantism and Liberty. Translated from the French by Wilfrid C. Robinson. 8vo., 1s.

Pale (The) and the Septs. A Romance of the XVI. Century. 6s.

Panegyrics of Fr. Segneri, S.J. Translated from the original Italian. With a Preface, by Rev. W. Humphrey, S.J. 12mo., 5s.

Paradise of God ; or the Virtues of the Sacred Heart. By Author of "God our Father," "Happiness of Heaven." 12mo., 4s.

Paray le Monial, and Bl. Margaret Mary. 18mo., 6d.

Passion of Our Lord, Harmony of. *See* Gayrard (Mme.).

PASSIONIST FATHERS : Mirror of Faith. 12mo., 3s.

  Manual of the Cross and Passion. 32mo., 3s.

  Sacred Eloquence. 18mo., 2s.

  S. Paul of the Cross. 12mo., 3s.

  School of Jesus Crucified. 18mo., 5s.

Pastor and People. By Rev. T. J. Potter. 12mo., 5s.

Path to Paradise. *See* Prayers, page 31.

Patrick (S.), Life of. 1s.; 8vo., 6s.; gilt, 10s.; 4to., 20s.

Patrick's (S.) Manual. By Miss Cusack. 18mo., 3s. 6d.
Patron Saints. By E. A. Starr. Illustrated. 12mo., 10s.
Paul of the Cross (S.), Life of. *See* Passionist Fathers.
Pearl among the Virtues. By Rev. P. A. De Doss. 12mo., 3s.
Penitential Psalms. *See* Blyth (Rev. F.).
PENS, Washbourne's Free and Easy. Fine, or Middle, or Broad Points, 1s. per gross.
People's Martyr. A Legend of Canterbury. 12mo., 4s.
Percy Grange. By Rev. T. J. Potter. 12mo., 3s.
Perpetual Adoration, Book of. Boudon. 12mo., 3s. and 3s. 6d.
Peter (S.), his Name and his Office. *See* Allies (T. W., Esq.).
Peter, Years of. By an ex-Papal Zouave. 12mo., 1d.
Philip Benizi (S.), Life of. *See* Oratorian Lives of the Saints.
Philomena (S.), Life and Miracles of. 12mo., 2s. 6d.
Philosophy, Elements of. By Rev. W. H. Hill. 8vo., 6s.
PHILPIN (Rev. F.), Holy Places; their sanctity and authenticity. With three Maps. 12mo., 2s. 6d. and 6s.
Photographs (10) illustrating the History of the Miraculous Hosts, called the Blessed Sacrament of the Miracle. 2s. 6d. the set.
Pius IX. 32mo., 6d.; 4to., 1d.
Pius IX., from his Birth to his Death. By G. White. 12mo., 6d.
Pius IX., his early Life to the Return from Gaeta. By Rev. T. B. Snow, O.S.B. 12mo., 6d.
Plain Chant. *See* Gregorian.
———— The Cecilian Society Music kept in stock.
PLATUS (Rev. F.), Origin and Progress of Religious Orders, and Happiness of a Religious State. 12mo., 2s. 6d.
PLAYS. *See* Dramas, page 10.
POIRIER (Bishop), A General Catechism of the Christian Doctrine. 18mo., 9d.
POOR CLARES OF KENMARE. *See* Cusack (Miss).
Pope-King, Rule of. By Rev. E. R. Martin. 8vo., 6d.
Pope of Rome. *See* Tondini (Rev. C.).
POTTER (Rev. T. J.), Extemporary Preaching. 5s.
———— Farleyes of Farleye. 12mo., 2s. 6d.
———— Pastor and People. 12mo., 5s.
———— Percy Grange. 12mo., 3s.
———— Rupert Aubrey. 12mo., 3s.
———— Sir Humphrey's Trial. 16mo., 2s. 6d.
POWELL (J., Esq.), Two Years in the Pontifical Zouaves. Illustrated. 8vo., 3s. 6d.
PRADEL (Fr., O. P.), Life of St. Vincent Ferrer. Translated by Rev. Fr. Dixon. With a Photograph. 12mo., 5s.
PRAYER BOOKS. *See* page 30.
PRINS (Leopold de). *See* Music.
Pro-Cathedral, Kensington. Tinted View of the Interior, 11 × 15 inches, 1s.; Proofs, on larger paper, 2s.
Prophecies, Contemporary. By Mgr. Dupanloup. 8vo., 1s.
Protestantism and Liberty. *See* Robinson (W. C.).
Protestant Principles examined by the Written Word. 1s.

Prussian Spy. A Novel. By V. Valmont. 12mo., 4s.

Purgatory, A Novena in favour of the Souls in. 32mo., 3d.

Purgatory, Month of the Souls in Purgatory. By Ricard, 1s.

Purgatory, The Doctrine of. By Rev. W. Marshall. 12mo., 1s.

Purgatory, Souls in. By Abbot Burder. 32mo., 3d.

Pusey's (Dr.) Eirenicon considered. *See* Oxenham (H. N.).

PYE (Henry John, M.A.), Necessity of Enquiry as to Religion. 32mo., 4d.; cloth, 6d.

—————— **The Religion of Common Sense.** New Edition. 1s.

—————— **Are the Ritualists Catholic?** 8vo., 6d.

RAMIERE (Rev. H.), Apostleship of Prayer. 12mo., 6s.

RAVIGNAN (Pere), The Spiritual Life, Conferences. Translated by Mrs. Abel Ram. 12mo., 5s.

Ravignan (Pere), Life of. 12mo., 9s.

RAWES (Rev F.), Homeward. 2s. **Sursum.** 1s.

Reading Lessons. By the Marist Brothers. 12mo., 1st Book, 4d.; 2nd Book, 7d.

REDMAN (Rev. Dr.), Book of Perpetual Adoration. By Mgr. Boudon. 12mo., 3s.; red edges, 3s. 6d.   [18mo., 1s.

REDMOND (Rev. Dr.), Eight Short Sermon Essays.

REEVE'S History of the Bible. 12mo., 3s. 6d.

Reflections, One Hundred Pious. *See* Butler.

Regina Sæculorum ; or, Mary Venerated in all Ages. Devotions to the Blessed Virgin from Ancient Sources. 12mo., 1s. and 3s.

Rejection of Catholic Doctrines attributable to the Non-Realization of Primary Truths. 8vo., 1s.

Religion of Common Sense. By H. J. Pye, M.A. 12mo., 1s.

Religious Orders. *See* Platus (Rev. F.).

Rest, on the Cross. By Eleanora Louisa Hervey. 12mo., 3s. 6d.

Reverse of the Medal. A Drama for Girls. 12mo., 6d.

RIBADENEIRA—Life, Passion, Death and Resurrection of our Lord. 12mo., 1s.

RICARD (Abbe), Month of the Holy Angels. 18mo., 1s.

—————— **Month of the Souls in Purgatory.** 18mo., 1s.

RICHARDSON (Rev. Fr.), Catholic Sick and Benefit Club; or, the Guild of our Lady; and St. Joseph's Catholic Burial Society. 32mo., 4d.

—————— **Little by Little** ; or, the Penny Bank. 32mo., 1d.

—————— **Shamrocks.** 6s. 2d. a gross (144), post free.

—————— **S. Joseph's Catholic Burial Society.** 2d.

—————— **The Crusade** ; or, Catholic Association for the Suppression of Drunkenness. 32mo., 1d.

Ritus Servandus in Expositione et Benedictione S.S. 4to., cloth, 5s. 6d.

Road to Heaven. A Game. By Miss M. A. Macdaniel. 3s. 6d.

ROBERTSON (Professor), Lectures on the Life, Writings, and Times of Edmund Burke. 12mo., 3s. 6d.

—————— **Lectures on Modern History and Biography.** 6s.

ROBINSON (Wilfrid C.), Protestantism and Liberty. Translated from the French of Professor Ozanam. 8vo., 1s.

Roman Question, The. By Rev. Dr. Husenbeth. 8vo., 6d.

Rome and her Captors : Letters collected and edited by Count Henri d'Ideville, and Translated by F. R. Wegg-Prosser. 4s.

Rome, Past, Present, and Future. By Dr. M'Corry. 8vo., 6d.
———— Personal Recollections of. By W. J. Jacob, 8vo., 6d.
———— The Victories of. By Rev. F. Beste. 8vo., 1s.
———— (To) and Back. Fly-Leaves from a Flying Tour. Edited by Rev. W. H. Anderdon, S.J., 12mo., 2s.
Rosalie ; or, the Memoir of a French Child, told by herself. 12mo., 1s.; stronger bound, 1s. 6d.; gilt, 2s.
Rosary, Fifteen Mysteries of, and Fourteen Stations of the Cross. In One Volume, 32 Illustrations. 16mo., 2s.
Rosary for the Souls in Purgatory, with Indulgenced Prayer. 6d. and 9d. Medals separately, 1d. each, or 9s. gross. Prayers separately, 1d. each, 9d. a dozen, or 6s. for 100.
Rosary, Chats about the. *See* Aunt Margaret's Little Neighbours.
ROWLEY (Rev. Austin John), A Devout Exposition of the Holy Mass. Composed by John Heigham. 12mo., 4s.
RUSSELL (Rev. M.) Eucharistic Verses. 12mo., 2s.
RUTTER (Rev. H.) Life and Sufferings of Our Lord, with Introduction by Rev. Dr. Husenbeth. Illustrated. 12mo., 5s.
RYAN (Bishop) What Catholics do not Believe. 12mo., 1s.
Sacred Heart, Act of Consecration to. 1d.; or 6s. per 100.
——————————, Act of Reparation to. 1s. 2d. per 100.
——————————, A Spiritual Banquet. 6d.
——————————, Devotions to. By Rev. S. Franco. 12mo., 4s.; cheap edition, 2s. [cloth, 6d.; gilt, 1s.
——————————, Devotions to. By Bishop Milner. 32mo., 3d.;
——————————, Devotions to. Translated by Rev. J. Joy Dean. 12mo., 2s. [12mo., 3s.
——————————, Elevations to the. By Rev. Fr. Doyotte, S.J.
——————————, Handbook of the Confraternity, for the use of Members. 18mo., 3d.
——————————, Little Treasury of. 32mo., 2s.; French morocco, 2s. 6d.; calf, 5s. ; morocco, 6s.
——————————, Manual of Devotions to the, from the writings of Blessed Margaret Mary. 32mo., 3d.
—————————— offered to the Piety of the Young engaged in Study. By Rev. F. Deham. 32mo., 6d.
—————————— *See* Paradise of God ; Kinane (Rev. T. H.).
—————————— Pleadings of. By Rev. M. Comerford. 18mo., 1s.; gilt edges, 2s.; with Handbook of the Confraternity, 1s. 6d.
——————————, Treasury of. 18mo., 3s. 6d.; roan, 4s.
Sacred History in Forty Pictures. Plain, 5s.; coloured, 7s. 6d.; mounted on cardboard, coloured, 18s. 6d. and 22s.
Saints, Lives of. By Alban Butler. 4 vols., 8vo., 32s.; gilt, 50s.; and leather, gilt, 64s.; or the 4 vols. in 2, 28s.; gilt, 34s.
——————————— for every day in the Year. Beautifully printed, within illustrated borders from ancient sources, on thick toned paper. 4to., gilt, 21s.
———— Patron. By E. A. Starr. Illustrated. 12mo., 10s.
ST. JURE (S.J.) Knowledge and Love of Jesus Christ. 3 vols., 8vo., 30s.
———— The Spiritual Man. 12mo., 6s.

R. Washbourne, 18 *Paternoster Row, London.*

Sanctuary Meditations for Priests and Frequent Communicants. Translated from the Spanish of Fr. Baltasar Gracian, by Mariana Monteiro. 12mo., 4s.

SCARAMELLI—Directorium Asceticum ; or, Guide to the Spiritual Life. 4 vols. 12mo., 24s. Vols. 4, 3, or 2 sold separately, 6s. each.

SCHMID (Canon), Tales. Illustrated. 12mo., 3s. 6d. Separately :—The Canary Bird, The Dove, The Inundation, The Rose Tree, The Water Jug, The Wooden Cross. 6d. each ; gilt, 1s.

SCHOOL BOOKS. Supplied according to order.

School of Jesus Crucified. By the Passionist Fathers. 18mo., 5s.

SCHOUVALOFF (Rev. Father, Barnabite), My Conversion and Vocation. Translated from the French, with an Appendix, by Fr. C. Tondini. 12mo., 5s.

SCHULTHES (William). *See* Music.

Scraps from my Scrapbook. *See* Arnold (M. J.).

SEGNERI (Fr., S.J.), Panegyrics. Translated from the original Italian. With a Preface, by Rev. W. Humphrey. 12mo., 5s.

SEGUR (Mgr.), Books for Little Children. Translated. 32mo., 3d. each. Confession, Holy Communion, Child Jesus, Piety, Prayer, Temptation and Sin. In one volume, cloth, 2s.

—————— **Practical Counsels for Holy Communion.** 18mo., 1s.

SEGUR (Countess de), The Little Hunchback. 12mo., 3s.

Seigneret (Paul), Life of. 12mo., 6d., 1s., and 1s. 6d.; gilt, 2s.

Selva ; a Collection of Matter for Sermons. By St. Liguori. 12mo., 5s.

Semi-Tropical Trifles. By H. Compton. 12mo., 1s.; cloth, 2s. 6d.

Sermon Essays. By Rev. Dr. Redmond. 12mo., 1s.

Sermons. Irish and English. By Dr. O'Gallagher. 8vo., 7s. 6d.

—————— By Father Burke, O.P., and others. 12mo., 2s.

——————— **The Light of the Holy Spirit in the World.** By Bishop Hedley. 1s.; cloth, 1s. 6d.

—————— **One Hundred Short.** By Rev. Fr. Thomas. 8vo., 12s.

Sermons, Lectures, &c. By Rev. M. M. Buckley. 12mo., 6s.

Serving Boy's Manual, and Book of Public Devotions. Containing all those prayers and devotions for Sundays and Holydays, usually divided in their recitation between the Priest and the Congregation. Compiled from approved sources, and adapted to Churches, served either by the Secular or Regular Clergy. 32mo., embossed, 1s.; French morocco, 2s.; calf, 4s.; with Epistles and Gospels, 6d. extra.

Seven Sacraments Explained and Defended. 18mo., 1s. 6d.

SHAKESPEARE. Expurgated edition. By Rosa Baughan. 8vo., 6s. The Comedies only, 3s. 6d.

Shandy Maguire. A Farce for Boys. 2 Acts. 12mo., 2s.

SHAW (T. H.), Holy Church the Centre of Unity ; or, Ritualism compared with Catholicism. 8vo., 1s.

Siege of Limerick (Florence O'Neill). *See* Stewart (Agnes M.).

SIGHART (Dr.) Albertus Magnus. 10s. 6d. Cheap edition, 5s.

Silver Teapot. By Elizabeth King. 18mo., 4d.

Simple Tales—Waiting for Father, &c., &c. 16mo., 2s. 6d.

Sir Ælfric and other Tales. *See* Bampfield (Rev. G.).

Sir Humphrey's Trial. By Rev. T. J. Potter. 16mo., 2s. 6d.

Sir Thomas Maxwell and his Ward. By Miss Bridges. 12mo, 1s. and 2s.

Sisters of Charity, Manual of. 18mo. 6s.

SMITH-SLIGO (A. V., Esq.), Life of the Ven. Anna Maria Taigi. Translated from French of Calixte. 8vo., 2s. 6d. and 5s.

— (Mrs.) Margarethe Verflassen. 12mo., 1s. 6d., 3s., and 3s. 6d.

SNOW (Rev. T. B.), Pius IX., His early Life to the Return from Gaeta. 12mo., 6d.

Soul (The), United to Jesus. 32mo., 1s. 6d.

SPALDING'S (Abp.) Works. 5 vols., 52s. 6d.; or separately Evidences of Catholicity, 10s. 6d.; Miscellanea, 2 vols., 21s.; Protestant Reformation, 2 vols., 21s.; cheap edition, 1 vol., 14s.

Spalding (Archbishop), Life of. 8vo., 10s. 6d.

———— Sermon at the Month's Mind. 8vo., 1s.

Spiritual Conferences on the Mysteries of Faith and the Interior Life. By Father Collins. 12mo., 5s.

Spiritual Life. Conferences by Père Ravignan. Translated by Mrs. Abel Ram. 12mo., 5s.

Spiritual Works of Louis of Blois. Edited by Rev. F. John Bowden. 12mo., 3s. 6d.; red edges, 4s.

Spouse of Christ. By Sister M. F. Clare. 12mo., vol. 2, 7s. 6d.

STARR (Eliza Allen), Patron Saints. Illustrated. 12mo., 10s.

Stations of the Cross, Devotions for Public and Private Use at the. By Miss Cusack. Illustrated. 16mo., 1s. and 1s. 6d.

Stations of the Cross. By S. Liguori. 18mo., 1d.

Stations of the Cross and Mysteries of the Rosary. 2s.

STEWART (A. M.), Alone in the World. 12mo., 4s. 6d.

———— St. Angela's Manual. *See* Angela (S.)

———— Biographical Readings. 12mo., 4s. 6d.

———— Cardinal Wolsey. 12mo., 6s. 6d.

———— Sir Thomas More. Illustrated, 10s. 6d.; gilt, 11s. 6d.

———— Life of S. Angela Merici. 12mo., 4s. 6d.

———— Life in the Cloister. 12mo., 3s. 6d. [extra, 6s.

———— Limerick Veteran; or, the Foster Sisters. 12mo., 5s.;

———— Margaret Roper. 12mo., 6s.; extra, 7s. [16mo., 1s.

Stories for my Children—The Angels and the Sacraments.

Stories of Holy Lives. By M. F. S. 12mo., 3s. 6d.

Stories of Martyr Priests. By M. F. S. 12mo., 3s. 6d.

Stories of the Saints. By M. F. S. 12mo., 1st Series, 3s. 6d.; gilt, 4s. 6d. 2nd Series, 3s. 6d.; gilt, 4s. 6d. 3rd Series, 3s. 6d.

Stormsworth, with other Poems and Plays. By the author of "Thy Gods, O Israel.' 12mo., 3s. 6d.

Story of an Orange Lodge. 12mo., 1s.

Story of Marie and other Tales. 12mo., 2s.; gilt, 3s., or separately :—The Story of Marie, 2d.; Nelly Blane, and a Contrast, 2d.; A Conversion and a Death-bed, 2d.; Herbert Montagu, 2d.; Jane Murphy, the Dying Gipsy, and the Nameless Grave, 2d.; The Beggars, and True and False Riches, 2d.; Pat and his Friend, 2d.

Story of the Life of St. Paul. By M. F. S., author of "Stories of the Saints." 12mo., 2s. 6d.

Sufferings of our Lord. Sermons preached by Father Claude de la Colombière, S.J., in the Chapel Royal, St. James's, in the year 1677. 18mo., 1s.; stronger bound, 1s. 6d.; red edges, 2s.

Supernatural Life, The. By Mgr. Mermillod. Translated from the French, with a Preface by Lady Herbert. 12mo., 5s.

Supremacy of the Roman See. By C. E. Tame, Esq. 8vo., 6d.

Sure Way to Heaven. A Little Manual for Confession and Holy Communion. 32mo., 6d.; Persian, 2s. 6d.; calf or morocco, 3s. 6d.

Sweetness of Holy Living ; or, Honey culled from the Flower Garden of S. Francis of Sales. 18mo., 1s.; French morocco, 3s.

Taigi (Anna Maria), Life of. Translated from the French of Calixte by A. V. Smith-Sligo, Esq. 8vo., 2s. 6d. and 5s.

Tales and Sketches. *See* Fleet (Charles).

Tales of the Jewish Church. By Charles Walker. 12mo., 2s. 6d.

TAME (C. E., Esq.), Early English Literature. 16mo., 2s. a vol. I. Our Lady's Lament, and the Lamentation of S. Mary Magdalene. II. Life of Our Lady, in verse.

———— **Supremacy of the Roman See.** 8vo., 6d.

TANDY (Rev. Dr.), Terry O'Flinn. 12mo., 1s.; stronger bound, 1s. 6d.; gilt, 2s.

TAUNTON (M.), Last of the Catholic O'Malleys. 18mo., 1s. 6d.; stronger bound, 2s.

———— **One Hundred Pious Reflections,** from Alban Butler's Lives of the Saints. 18mo., 1s.; stronger bound, 2s.

Temperance Books. *See* Richardson (Rev. Fr.).

———— Cards (Illuminated), 3d. each.   [3d. each.

———— Medals—Immaculate Conception, St. Patrick, St. Joseph.

Terry O'Flinn. By Rev. Dr. Tandy. 12mo., 1s., 1s. 6d. and 2s.

Testimony ; or, the Necessity of Enquiry as to Religion. By John Henry Pye, M.A. 32mo., 4d.; cloth, 6d.

THOMAS (H. J.), One Hundred Short Sermons. 8vo., 12s.

Three Wishes. A Tale. By M. F. S. 12mo., 2s 6d.

Threshold of the Catholic Church. *See* Bagshawe (Rev. J. B.)

Tim O'Halloran's Choice. *See* Cusack.

Tom's Crucifix, and other Tales. By M. F. S. 12mo., 3s., or in 5 vols., 1s. each; gilt, 1s. 6d.

TONDINI (Rev. Cæsarius), My Conversion and Vocation. By Rev. Fr. Schouvaloff. 12mo., 5s.

———— **The Pope of Rome and the Popes of the Oriental Orthodox Church.** An essay on Monarchy in the Church, with special reference to Russia. Second Edition. 12mo., 3s. 6d.

———— **Some Documents concerning of the Association Prayers in Honour of Mary Immaculate, for the Return of the Greek-Russian Church to Catholic Unity.** 12mo., 3d. Association of Prayers, 32mo., 1d.

Transubstantiation, Catholic Doctrine of. 12mo., 6d.

Trials of Faith. *See* Browne (E. G. K.).

TRONSON (Abbe), The Mass : a devout Method. 32mo., 4d.

TRONSON'S Conferences for Ecclesiastical Students and
 Religious. By Sister M. F. Clare. 12mo., 4s. 6d.
Two Colonels. By Father Thomas. 12mo., 6s. [gilt, 1s. 6d.
Two Friends ; or Marie's Self-Denial. By Madame d'Arras. 1s., or
 Ursuline Manual. *See* Prayers, page 32.
VALMONT (V.), The Prussian Spy. A Novel. 12mo., 4s.
VAUGHAN (Bishop of Salford), Holy Sacrifice of the
 Mass. 2d. ; cloth, 6d.
———— Love and Passion of Jesus Christ. 2d.
VERE (Rev. G. L.), The Catholic Hymn Book. 32mo.,
 2d.; cloth, 4d. Appendix containing Hymns in honour of Saints. 1d.
Veronica Giuliani (S.), Life of, and B. Battista Varani.
 With a Photographic Portrait. 12mo., 5s.
Village Lily. A Tale. 12mo., 1s.; gilt, 1s. 6d.
Vincent Ferrer (S.), of the Order of Friar Preachers ; his
 Life, Spiritual Teaching, and Practical Devotion.
 By Rev. Fr. Andrew Pradel, O.P. Translated from the French by
 the Rev. Fr. T. A. Dixon, O.P.. with a Photograph. 12mo., 5s.
VINCENT OF LIRINS (S.). Commonitory. 12mo., 1s. 3d.
Vincent of Paul (S.), Glory of. *See* Manning (Archbishop).
VIRGIL. Literally translated by Davidson. 12mo., 2s. 6d.
"Vitis Mystica" ; or, the True Vine. *See* Brownlow.
WALKER (Charles), Are You Safe in the Church of
 England ? 8vo., 6d.
———— Tales of the Jewish Church. 12mo., 2s. 6d.
WALLER (J. F., Esq.), Festival Tales. 12mo., 3s. 6d.
Way of Salvation. By S. Liguori. 32mo., 1s.
WEBB(Alfred), Compendium of Irish Biography. 8vo., 16s.
Weedall (Mgr.), Life of. By Rev. Dr. Husenbeth. 8vo., 1s.
WEGG-PROSSER (F. R.), Rome and her Captors. 4s.
Wenefred (St.), Life of. By Rev. T. Meyrick. 12mo., 2s.
What Catholics do not Believe. By Bishop Ryan. 12mo., 1s.
WENINGER (Rev. F.X., S.J.), Lives of the Saints for every
 day in the Year. Illustrated. 4to., 2 vols., or 12 vols., 50s.
WHITE (George), Cardinal Wiseman. 12mo., 1s. and 1s. 6d.
———— Comte de Montalembert. 12mo., 6d.
———— Life of S. Edmund of Canterbury. 1s. and 1s. 6d.
———— Pius IX., from his Birth to his Death. 12mo., 6d.
William (St.), of York. A Drama in Two Acts. (Boys.) 12mo., 6d.
WILLIAMS (Canon), Anglican Orders. 12mo., 3s. 6d.
Wiseman (Cardinal), Life and Obsequies. 1s. and 1s. 6d.
———— Recollections of. By M. J. Arnold. 12mo., 2s. 6d.
WOODS (Canon), Defence of the Roman Church against
 F. Gratry. Translated from the French of Gueranger. 1s. 6d.
WYATT-EDGELL (Alfred), Stormsworth, with other Poems
 and Plays. 12mo., 3s. 6d.
———— Thy Gods ! O Israel. 12mo., 2s.
Young Catholic's Guide to Confession and Holy Com-
 munion. By Dr. Kenny. 32mo., 4d.; cloth, 6d.; red edges, 9d.,
 French morocco, 1s. 6d.; calf or morocco, 2s. 6d.
YOUNG (T., Esq.), History of Ireland. 18mo., 2s. 6d.
Zouaves, Pontifical, Two Years in. By Joseph Powell, Z.P.
 Illustrated. 8vo., 3s. 6d.

R Washbourne, 18 *Paternoster Row, London.*

PRAYER BOOKS.

Garden, Little, of the Soul. Edited by the Rev. R. G. Davis. *With Imprimatur of the Archbishop of Westminster.* This book, as its name imports, contains a selection from the "Garden of the Soul" of the Prayers and Devotions of most general use. Whilst it will serve as a *Pocket Prayer Book* for all, it is, by its low price, *par excellence*, the Prayer Book for children and for the very poor. In it are to be found the old familiar Devotions of the "Garden of the Soul," as well as many important additions, such as the Devotions to the Sacred Heart, to Saint Joseph, to the Guardian Angels, and others. The omissions are mainly the Forms of administering the Sacraments, and Devotions that are not of very general use. It is printed in a clear type, on a good paper, both especially selected, for the purpose of obviating the disagreeableness of small type and inferior paper. Fifteenth Thousand.

32mo., price, cloth, **6d.**; with rims, 1s. Embossed, red edges, 9d.; with rims and clasp, 1s. 3d.; Strong roan, 1s.; with rims and clasp, 1s. 6d. French morocco, 1s. 6d.; with rims and clasp, 2s. French morocco extra gilt, 2s.; with rims and clasp, 2s. 6d. Calf or morocco, 3s.; with rims and clasp, 4s. Calf or morocco, extra gilt, 4s.; with rims and clasp, 5s. Morocco antique, 7s. 6d., 10s. 6d., 12s., 16s. Velvet, rims and clasp, 5s., 8s. 6d., and 10s. 6d. Russia, 5s.; with clasp, &c., 8s.; Russia antique, 17s. 6d. Ivory, with rims and clasp, 10s. 6d., 13s., 15s., 17s. 6d. Imitation ivory, with rims and clasp, 3s. With oxydized silver or gilt mountings, in morocco case, 25s.

Catholic Hours : a Manual of Prayer, including Mass and Vespers. By J. R. Digby Beste, Esq. 32mo., cloth, 2s.; red edges, 2s. 6d.; roan, 3s.; morocco, 6s.

Catholic Piety ; or, Key of Heaven, with Epistles and Gospels. Large 32mo., roan, 1s. 6d. and 2s.; French morocco, with rims and clasp, 2s. 6d.; extra gilt, 3s.; with rims and clasp, 3s. 6d.

Catholic Piety ; or, Key of Heaven. 32mo., 6d.; rims and clasp, 1s.; French morocco, 1s.; velvet, with rims and clasp, 2s. 6d.; with Epistles and Gospels, roan, 1s.; French morocco, 1s. 6d.; with rims and clasp, 2s.; extra gilt, 2s.; Persian, 2s. 6d.; imitation ivory, 3s.; morocco, 3s. 6d.; velvet, rims and clasp, 3s. 6d.

Crown of Jesus. 18mo., Persian calf, 6s. Calf or Morocco, 7s. 6d. and 8s. 6d.; with rims and clasp, 10s. 6d. Calf or morocco, extra gilt, 10s. 6d.; with rims and clasp, 12s. 6d; with turn-over edges, 10s. 6d. Ivory, with rims and clasp, 21s., 25s., 27s. 6d. and 30s.

Daily Exercises for Devout Christians. By Rev. P. V. Monk, O.S.B. 18mo., 3s. 6d.

Devotions for Mass. Very large type, 12mo., 2d.

Garden of the Soul. Very large Type. 18mo., cloth, 1s.; with Epistles and Gospels, 1s. 6d.; French morocco, 2s. 6d.; with E. and G., 3s. 6d. Best edition, without E. and G., 3s. 6d.; with E. and G., morocco circuit, 7s. 6d.; calf antique, with clasp, 8s.; French morocco, antique, with clasp, 6s. 6d.

Epistles and Gospels, in French morocco, 2s.

R. Washbourne, 18 *Paternoster Row, London.*

Holy Childhood. Simple Prayers for very little children. 32mo., 1s.; gilt, 1s. 6d. ; cheap edition, 6d.

Illustrated Manual of Prayers. 32mo., 3d.; cloth, 4d.

Key of Heaven. *Very large type.* 18mo., 1s. ; leather, 2s. 6d.

Lily of St. Joseph, The ; a little Manual of Prayers and Hymns for Mass. 64mo., price 2d.; cloth, 3d., 4d., 6d., or 8d.; roan, 1s.; French morocco, 1s. 6d.; calf or morocco, 2s.; gilt, 2s. 6d.

Little Prayer Book, The, for Ordinary Catholic Devotions. 3d.

Manual of Catholic Devotions. Small, for the waistcoat pocket. 64mo., 6d.; with Epistles and Gospels, cloth, 6d.; with rims, 1s.; roan, 1s.; with tuck, 1s. 6d. ; calf or morocco, 2s. 6d.; ivorine, 2s. 6d.

Manual of Devotions in Honour of our Lady of Sorrows. 18mo., 1s. 6d.; cheaper binding, 1s.

Manual of the Sisters of Charity. 18mo., 6s.

Memorare Mass. By Sister M. F. Clare, of Kenmare. 32mo., 2d.

Missal (Complete). 18mo., Persian, 8s. 6d.; calf or morocco, 10s. 6d.; with rims and clasp, 13s. 6d.; calf or mor., extra gilt, 12s. 6d., with rims and clasp, 15s. 6d.; morocco, with turn-over edges, 13s. 6d. ; morocco antique, 15s. ; velvet, 20s.; Russia, 20s.; ivory, with rims and clasp, 31s. 6d. and 35s.

——— A very beautiful edition, handsomely bound in morocco, gilt mountings, silk linings, edges red on gold, in a morocco case. Illustrated, £5. [clasp, 8s.

Missal and Vesper Book, in one vol. 32mo., morocco, 6s.; with

Occasional Prayers for Festivals. 4d. and 6d.; gilt, 1s.

OREMUS, A Liturgical Prayer Book : with the Imprimatur of the Cardinal Archbishop of Westminster. An adaptation of the Church Offices : containing Morning and Evening Devotions ; Devotion for Mass, Confession, and Communion, and various other Devotions ; Common and Proper, Hymns, Lessons, Collects, Epistles and Gospels for Sundays, Feasts, and Week Days ; and short notices of over 200 Saints' Days. 32mo., 452 pages, 2s. ; cloth, 2s. 6d.; embossed, red edges, 3s. 6d.; French morocco, 4s. 6d.; calf, 5s. 6d.; morocco, 6s.; Russia, 8s. 6d., &c., &c., &c.

Path to Paradise. 32 full-page Illustrations. 32mo., cloth, 3d. With 50 Illustrations, cloth, 4d. Superior edition, 6d. and 1s.

Serving Boy's Manual and Book of Catholic Devotions, containing all those Prayers and Devotions for Sundays and Holidays, usually divided in their recitation between the Priest and the Congregation. Compiled from approved sources, and adapted to Churches served either by the Secular or the Regular Clergy, 32mo., Embossed, 1s.; with Epistles and Gospels, 1s. 6d.; French morocco, 2s., with Epistles and Gospels, 2s. 6d.; calf, 4s., with Epistles and Gospels, 4s. 6d.

Soul united to Jesus in the Adorable Sacrament. 1s. 6d.

S. Patrick's Manual. Compiled by Sister Mary Frances Clare. 3s. 6d.

Sure Way to Heaven. Cloth, 6d. : Persian, 2s. 6d.; morocco, 3s. 6d.

Treasury of the Sacred Heart. 18mo., 3s. 6d.; roan, 4s. 6d. 32mo., 2s.; French morocco, 2s. 6d. ; calf 5s.; morocco, 6s.

Ursuline Manual. 18mo., 4s.; Persian calf, 7s. 6d.; morocco, 10s.

R. Washbourne, 18 *Paternoster Row, London.*

Garden of the Soul. (WASHBOURNE'S EDITION.)   Edited by the Rev. R. G. Davis.   *With Imprimatur of the Archbishop of Westminster.*   Twentieth Thousand.   This Edition retains all the Devotions that have made the GARDEN OF THE SOUL, now for many generations, the well-known Prayer-book for English Catholics. During many years various Devotions have been introduced, and, in the form of appendices, have been added to other editions. These have now been incorporated into the body of the work, and, together with the Devotions to the Sacred Heart, to Saint Joseph, to the Guardian Angels, the Itinerarium, and other important additions, render this edition pre-eminently the Manual of Prayer, for both public and private use.   The version of the Psalms has been carefully revised, and strictly conformed to the Douay translation of the Bible, published with the approbation of the LATE CARDINAL WISEMAN.   The Forms of administering the Sacraments have been carefully translated, *as also the rubrical directions*, from the Ordo Administrandi Sacramenta.   To enable all present, either at baptisms or other public administrations of the Sacraments, to pay due attention to the sacred rites, the Forms are inserted without any curtailment, both in Latin and English.   The Devotions at Mass have been carefully revised, and enriched by copious adaptations from the prayers of the Missal.   The preparation for the Sacraments of Penance and the Holy Eucharist have been the objects of especial care, to adapt them to the wants of those whose religious instruction may be deficient.   Great attention has been paid to the quality of the paper and to the size of type used in the printing, to obviate that weariness so distressing to the eyes, caused by the use of books printed in small close type and on inferior paper.

32mo.   Embossed, 1s. ; with rims and clasp, 1s. 6d. ; with Epistles and Gospels, 1s. 6d. ; with rims and clasp, 2s.   French morocco, 2s. ; with rims and clasp, 2s. 6d. ; with E. and G., 2s. 6d. ; with rims and clasp, 3s.   French morocco extra gilt, 2s. 6d. ; with rims and clasp, 3s. ; with E. and G., 3s. ; with rims and clasp, 3s. 6d.   Calf, or morocco 4s. ; with rims and clasp, 5s. 6d. ; with E. and G., 4s. 6d., with rims and clasp, 6s.   Calf or morocco extra gilt, 5s. ; with rims and 'clasp, 6s. 6d. ; with E. and G., 5s. 6d. ; with rims and clasp, 7s.   Velvet, with rims and clasp, 7s. 6d., 10s. 6d., and 13s. ; with E. and G., 8s., 11s., and 13s. 6d. Russia, antique, with clasp, 8s. 6d., 10s., 12s. 6d. ; with E. and G., 9s. 10s. 6d., 13s., with corners and clasps, 20s. ; with E. and G. 20s. 6d. Ivory 14s., 16s., 18s., 20s., and 22s. 6d. ; with E. and G., 14s. 6d., 16s. 6d., 18s. 6d., 20s. 6d., and 23s.   Morocco antique, with 2 patent clasps, 12s. ; with E. and G., 12s. 6d. ; with corners and clasps, 18s. ; with E.and G., 18s. 6d.

The Epistles and Gospels.   *Complete*, cloth, 6d. ; roan, 1s. 6d.

"This is one of the best editions we have seen of one of the best of all our Prayer Books. It is well printed in clear, large type, on good paper."—*Catholic Opinion*. A very complete arrangement of this which is emphatically the Prayer Book of every Catholic household. It is as cheap as it is good, and we heartily recommend it."—*Universe*. "Two striking features are the admirable order displayed throughout the book, and the insertion of the Indulgences in small type above Indulgenced Prayers. In the Devotions for Mass, the editor has, with great discrimination, drawn largely on the Church's Prayers, as given us in the Missal."—*Weekly Register.*

R. Washbourne, 18 *Paternoster Row, London.*

www.ingramcontent.com/pod-product-compliance
Lightning Source LLC
Chambersburg PA
CBHW020615030726
47497CB00007B/2250